Exhortation to Understand and to Keep the Faith

SEBASTIAN IYERE

authorHOUSE®

AuthorHouse™
1663 Liberty Drive
Bloomington, IN 47403
www.authorhouse.com
Phone: 1-800-839-8640

First published by AuthorHouse   01/11/2012

ISBN: 978-1-4678-8309-2 (sc)
ISBN: 978-1-4678-8308-5 (ebk)

Printed in the United States of America

Any people depicted in stock imagery provided by Thinkstock are models, and such images are being used for illustrative purposes only.
Certain stock imagery © Thinkstock.

This book is printed on acid-free paper.

Table of Contents

1 Developing the right personality for a lasting relationship 1

   1.1   Introduction 1

   1.2   Isaac: understood why he should not marry a
Canaanite 2

   1.3   Isaac: loved sincerely by his servant 8

   1.4   Isaac: accepted father's and servant's decision 12

   1.5   Isaac: readiness and timing 14

   1.6   Isaac: a man who walked with God, a man of
prayer 17

   1.7   Rebekah: a domestic sister 20

   1.8   Rebekah: physically fit 23

   1.9   Rebekah: skillful sister 26

   1.10 Rebekah: a helping sister 27

   1.11 Rebekah: the submissive sister...................................32

   1.12 Joseph and Mary: an example of an engaged
and married couple 34

   1.3   Mending the fence 45

2 Questions about money in the church.............................47

   2.1   Introduction...47

   2.2   Speaking out the truth..48

   2.3   Tithe..54

   2.4   Giving alms and offerings: Jesus and early
church era 72

   2.5   Vows 90

   2.6   Conclusion...92

3 Will He find faith on the earth when He returns?.................94

   3.1   Introduction...94

   3.2   Light and Salt..94

   3.3   Bad children..99

   3.4   Good children...103

   3.5   Conclusion...106

Introduction

As a Christian since the age of twelve, I have had to reappraise my beliefs and values over the years. This led me to read many books. Some were quite interesting, and some had an invaluable influence in my life. As I have grown older, I have come to understand that some of the authors of the Christian books I read over the years have written their books for personal profit. This indeed has been disturbing. While the apostle Paul would say that 'Christ is being preached' all the same, it is difficult for me to understand this pretext. Therefore, even before publishing this book, I decided that if I ever become a published Christian author, the profit must go to charity, and indeed that is the case with this book.

It has also been unsettling to see some of the values I held to so highly gradually being eroded. For example, it is not uncommon to hear of divorces or funds mismanagement among leaders in the church. This is the burden behind this book. It is to look at some fundamentals of Christian understanding. From my discussions with many people—friends, colleagues, and fellow church members—I know that many people are as disturbed as I am. I have chosen to address three issues in this book:

Developing the Right Personality for a Lasting Relationship

The first section re-evaluates the role of character in keeping relationships. This is an encouragement to focus on inner self in order to build successful relationships and homes, the way it was meant to be from the beginning.

Questions about Money in the Church

The second section helps us reappraise the current wave of prosperity teachers and focus on perfect religion (James 1:27), which is humanity and holy living.

Will He Find Faith on the Earth When He Returns?

The third and final section dwells on the ability to stand up for what we believe in. It encourages us to shine as light in this world (Matt. 5:16).

Genuine questions are asked in this book, with the hopes of finding answers. Or at least, making it known that there is someone out there who is truthfully seeking answers. It is my sincere belief that we must know the faith that has been delivered to us so we can contend for and keep it.

Developing the right personality for a lasting relationship

1.1   Introduction

This section on *Developing the Right Personality for a Lasting Relationship* looks at the role of personality in finding a partner and in living with one. We shall look at who is ready in character before marriage as well as living together after marriage. We understand that a church is strong only if homes making up the church are strong. Making the best home depends not only on prayer but also on personality. If we build the right spirit at home, we will drastically reduce the amount of praying we need to do and increase the efficacy of our prayers. We shall be using the examples of Isaac and Rebekah for unmarried brethren, and Joseph and Mary for married brethren.

The book dwells on their stories, showing what happened. It helps us to ask ourselves whether we would have behaved the same way. It explores what could have been on the minds of the characters in the stories. As we focus on particular scenes, the questions below are answered, amongst many others.

- How should we decide whom to marry?
- Do we have enough moral strength to treat everyone equally, including our subordinates and the less privileged?
- Are we ready for marriage? If not, should we wait until we are ready?
- How do we treat ideas and suggestions from other people, regardless of our pride?

- Do we still think that we can get all we need by power and might?
- Are we ready for the chores and skills involved in keeping a home?
- As wives, are we ready to submit to authority?
- As husbands, can we love selflessly?
- Have we kept long-time or childhood friendships?

Until we look at our mindsets and assure ourselves of our readiness to face these issues, we may want to delay marriage. We cannot be without opinions on these issues. To drift is more dangerous. We must make up our minds on sound doctrines.

1.2 Isaac: understood why he should not marry a Canaanite

And Esau was forty years old when he took to wife Judith the daughter of Beeri the Hittite, and Bashemath the daughter of Elon the Hittite: Which were a grief of mind unto Isaac and to Rebekah. (Gen. 26:34-35 KJV)

And Rebekah said to Isaac, I am weary of my life because of the daughters of Heth: if Jacob take a wife of the daughters of Heth, such as these which are of the daughters of the land, what good shall my life do me? (Gen. 27:46 KJV)

Arise, go to Padanaram, to the house of Bethuel thy mother's father; and take thee a wife from thence of the daughters of Laban thy mother's brother. And God Almighty bless thee, and make thee fruitful, and multiply thee, that thou mayest be a multitude of people; And give thee the blessing of Abraham, to thee, and to thy seed with thee; that thou mayest inherit the land wherein thou art a stranger, which God gave unto Abraham. And Isaac sent away Jacob: and he went to Padanaram unto Laban, son of Bethuel the Syrian, the brother of Rebekah, Jacob's and Esau's mother.

When Esau saw that Isaac had blessed Jacob, and sent him away to Padanaram, to take him a wife from thence; and that as he blessed

> *him he gave him a charge, saying, Thou shalt not take a wife of the daughters of Canaan; And that Jacob obeyed his father and his mother, and was gone to Padanaram; And Esau seeing that the daughters of Canaan pleased not Isaac his father; Then went Esau unto Ishmael, and took unto the wives which he had Mahalath the daughter of Ishmael Abraham's son, the sister of Nebajoth, to be his wife.* (Gen. 28:2-9 KJV)

From the above passages, Isaac's position about the Canaanites is clear. As the Bible says:

> *Train up a child in the way he should go: and when he is old, he will not depart from it.* (Prov. 22:6 KJV)

Abraham must have told Isaac this in many ways:

> *Be ye not unequally yoked together with unbelievers: for what fellowship hath righteousness with unrighteousness? and what communion hath light with darkness? And what concord hath Christ with Belial? or what part hath he that believeth with an infidel? And what agreement hath the temple of God with idols? for ye are the temple of the living God; as God hath said, I will dwell in them, and walk in them; and I will be their God, and they shall be my people.* (2 Cor. 6:14-16 KJV)

At forty, the same age as Esau, he consented to marrying a wife of the people of promise. Think about it: the only way Jacob could be excused to travel to Laban was to lie using this understanding. Esau could barely please his parents after he married a Canaanite. He needed to marry the daughter of Ishmael to get applause. Isaac probably married a child of promise to please his dad and God or because he saw it as the right thing to do. In any case, it is worth emulating, to marry a Christian if you are a Christian. Being people of promise with like minds is such a value in the home. Think about Rebekah. When she realized that there was war in her womb, she went to God to pray. If we marry Canaanites, they will go to their gods when the wind of life blows. Mind you, it will always blow. If both parties do not have the same god, then a division may be created.

How do we have a Christian home if the devil has an agent in the house? It is hard to fight with an enemy within. Isaac understood this: he was meditating when Rebekah came. Who says only the servant was praying? Isaac foresaw what would happen to people like Samson.

> And Samson went down to Timnath, and saw a woman in Timnath of the daughters of the Philistines. And he came up, and told his father and his mother, and said, I have seen a woman in Timnath of the daughters of the Philistines: now therefore get her for me to wife. Then his father and his mother said unto him, Is there never a woman among the daughters of thy brethren, or among all my people, that thou goest to take a wife of the uncircumcised Philistines? And Samson said unto his father, Get her for me; for she pleaseth me well. (Judg. 14:1-3 KJV)

We all know today the unpleasant end of Samson. Isaac made up his mind as to whom to marry. Marry from a family who worships God rather than a foreign woman so that, unlike wise Solomon, your heart is not turned away from God. Isaac did not want anything to draw his heart away from God. With all his wisdom, Solomon could not withstand the power of a wife, the power of a foreign god inside his home. Light and darkness in a home can be complicated, as stated in the Bible.

> Be not deceived: evil communications corrupt good manners. (1 Cor. 15:33 KJV)

Have we ever asked ourselves what it was that Solomon's wives said to convince a man full of glory and wisdom to turn him away from the God of Israel? Could God not have forced Solomon to avoid such a woman or to overcome her? Perhaps it is as a lesson to us so we are aware that God cannot force Himself on our choices as men. Did He not tell the Israelites not to marry the people whose land they were going to take over? We cannot demand more from Him.

At forty, Isaac must have heard stories about Sodom and Gomorrah, how God destroyed them. He also must have heard how God would not do anything without first telling His friend Abraham. He must have known why: he was trusted by Him to bring up the children in a godly way. How could a man who grew up in a godly home where the woman calls her husband lord require less? Oh, that parents should give their children homes where they can grow in wisdom and in stature and in favour with God and man. If only parents would show their children good examples. Until we as Christians all make up our minds to marry from the household of God, we will never have good marriages in the church. Success in marriages is based on values. Nothing less, nothing more. Let me explain. Have you ever wondered why bad people sometimes have wives who are ready to die for them, or whom they are ready to die for? No matter who you are, no matter what you do, from criminals to saints, from assassins to leaders, someone out there likes your values and spirit and may even love you. Love is based on likeness. In turn, likeness is solely dependent on values, and this is what makes a good home. There is this misconception by many that love is either mystical or sexual. Nothing could be further from the truth.

Some believe it is mystical because they believe that once you meet someone, you just love the person: love at first sight. However, these same people, if they face the truth, will tell you of one or two past meetings with people that probably started the same way. These past relationships didn't work out. How do we mean that such a 'mystical' union did not work out? It leaves us to wonder what else will work out. However, if we take time to dwell on this mystical love, we find out that, in truth, it was just based on initial values discovered. Maybe it was based on neatness, manner of dressing, choice of colours, walking style, accent, intellect displayed that very first time. It could even be a person's stature, hair colour, and so forth. In our subconscious minds, we all have images of our would-be partners. Once someone meets that person, one's likeness shoots up like the stars. This initial attraction must not be mistaken to be mystical. We as Christians look into the law of liberty, changing our values to conform to things above and not on the earth. In time, we form our own biblical values. We will never find all our values in one person. We must be ready to know which are vital to us and which we can do without. The truth is, people show their true colours, and impressions are created over time. If eventually such an impression is something we cherish, we like the person. At this point, we decide to be close to this person and overlook any weaknesses. This is, to me, love: the point where we decide to like the person given his strength and weakness. Let us not mystify love, for it erodes our responsibility and makes us think everything is magical. We must consciously maintain this decision to overlook weaknesses. We have the responsibility to plant, water, and keep love. If we visit the happy homes today (happy being by any definition; no infidelity, no quarrelling over money, no shouting, and so forth), whether these homes are Christian's or non-Christian's, we find out that the secret crystallizes to values appreciated in each other and conscious efforts to focus more on strength rather than weaknesses of the partner. Far be it that such love is based entirely on mysticism or mere sex.

Talking about sex, some believe that love is based on sex. Then you hear of things like 'lovemaking' replacing sex. Have they forgotten that sex is natural? Should we forget that the scriptures say that animals can have sex with humans and humans with animals? As early as the time of Moses, laws were made regarding this in Leviticus. Who says that sexual decadence is only for our age?

Neither shalt thou lie with any beast to defile thyself therewith: neither shall any woman stand before a beast to lie down thereto: it is confusion. Defile not ye yourselves in any of these things: for in all these the nations are defiled which I cast out before you: And the land is defiled: therefore I do visit the iniquity thereof upon it, and the land itself vomiteth out her inhabitants. Ye shall therefore keep my statutes and my judgments, and shall not commit any of these abominations; neither any of your own nation, nor any stranger that sojourneth among you: (For all these abominations have the men of the land done, which were before you, and the land is defiled;) That the land spue not you out also, when ye defile it, as it spued out the nations that were before you. For whosoever shall commit any of these abominations, even the souls that commit them shall be cut off from among their people. Therefore shall ye keep mine ordinance, that ye commit not any one of these abominable customs, which were committed before you, and that ye defile not yourselves therein: I am the LORD your God. (Lev. 18:23-30 KJV)

And if a man lie with a beast, he shall surely be put to death: and ye shall slay the beast. And if a woman approach unto any beast, and lie down thereto, thou shalt kill the woman, and the beast: they shall surely be put to death; their blood shall be upon them. (Lev. 20:15-16 KJV)

As if that is not enough, angels and demons can even have sex with humans.

And it came to pass, when men began to multiply on the face of the earth, and daughters were born unto them, That the sons of God saw the daughters of men that they were fair; and they took them wives of all which they chose. (Gen. 1:1-2 KJV)

So where does sex come in? How do we 'make love' with animals? Is sex just a natural urge that needs to be fulfilled, whether in animals or in humans? Or do we describe raping as 'making love'? In some animals, sex is only for reproduction. In humans and some other animals, it is a social thing. The scripture is clear that a mother can have sex with a son. Look at the scripture that indicates that sexual activities with close relatives.

None of you shall approach to any that is near of kin to him, to uncover their nakedness: I am the LORD. The nakedness of thy father, or the nakedness of thy mother, shalt thou not uncover: she is thy mother; thou shalt not uncover her nakedness. The nakedness of thy father's wife shalt thou not uncover: it is thy father's nakedness. The nakedness of thy sister, the daughter of thy father, or daughter of thy mother, whether she be born at home, or born abroad, even their nakedness thou shalt not uncover. The nakedness of thy son's daughter, or of thy daughter's daughter, even their nakedness thou shalt not uncover: for theirs is thine own nakedness. The nakedness of thy father's wife's daughter, begotten of thy father, she is thy sister, thou shalt not uncover her nakedness. Thou shalt not uncover the nakedness of thy father's sister: she is thy father's near kinswoman.

> *Thou shalt not uncover the nakedness of thy mother's sister: for she is thy mother's near kinswoman. Thou shalt not uncover the nakedness of thy father's brother, thou shalt not approach to his wife: she is thine aunt. Thou shalt not uncover the nakedness of thy daughter in law: she is thy son's wife; thou shalt not uncover her nakedness. Thou shalt not uncover the nakedness of thy brother's wife: it is thy brother's nakedness. Thou shalt not uncover the nakedness of a woman and her daughter, neither shalt thou take her son's daughter, or her daughter's daughter, to uncover her nakedness; for they are her near kinswomen: it is wickedness. Neither shalt thou take a wife to her sister, to vex her, to uncover her nakedness, beside the other in her life time.* (Lev. 18:6-18 KJV)

Do we not see that sex can virtually happen with any opposite sex? It can happen with the same sexual excitement given the same physical touch. So when people see love and sex as the same thing, it is totally what the Bible calls it: sexual perversion. Period.

Wrapping it up let us say that when we marry people based on biblical values, one of which is that both of us are of God, we can say confidently that we are on the path to a happy home. At the very least, since the Holy Spirit is working in us, He will make us willing and ready to do what pleases Him.

When I was growing up, I once asked one of my Sunday school teachers why one cannot marry a non-Christian with the hope that the partner will eventually be saved. He simply answered, 'There are some people who will never be saved, and your choice might just be one of those people. You will not like it now and hereafter.'

1.3   Isaac: loved sincerely by his servant

One cannot overlook the astounding strength of character here. To fully understand, we need to ask ourselves some questions. Why would the centurion come to Jesus neither for a sick son nor a father but for a servant? Why would Onesimus run away from Philemon? Why would the Holy Spirit record it? Why would Gehazi, Elisha's servant, go for money? Why is it that God allowed servants to have the option of staying with their masters forever? Why would a servant hide Jonathan's son? Why would the little servant girl tell Naaman that there was a prophet in Israel and expect the God of her fathers to hear him? We could continue to ask ourselves thousands of questions especially when it is only by so doing that we can understand this personality.

As we go through this chapter, we shall consider the words servant, younger ones, maids, employees, lower ranks, and subordinates to mean the same thing.

Let us start with Philemon and his servant Onesimus. Paul and indeed the Holy Spirit bore witness to this man's spirit.

> *Paul, a prisoner of Jesus Christ, and Timothy our brother, unto Philemon our dearly beloved, and fellow labourer, And to our beloved Apphia, and Archippus our fellow soldier, and to the church in thy house: Grace to you, and peace, from God our Father and the Lord Jesus Christ. I thank my God, making mention of thee always in my prayers, Hearing of thy love and faith, which thou hast toward the Lord Jesus, and toward all saints; That the communication of thy faith may become effectual by the acknowledging of every good thing which is in you in Christ Jesus. For we have great joy and consolation in thy love, because the bowels of the saints are refreshed by thee, brother. (Philem. 1-6 KJV)*

- He was dearly beloved.
- He was a fellow labourer.
- He had a beloved wife.
- He had a fellow soldier of the cross as a son.
- He had a church in his house.
- He had someone always praying for him.
- He had love and faith towards God and the saints.
- He refreshed the bowels of the saints.

The Bible says Philemon was a wonderful man, full of faith, love, and hospitality. Is it not shocking to see that this man had a rebellious servant at home? Clearly he did not rebel because the man was a

Christian full of too much love. He would not have run away. A man full of love would be approachable. The servant could have asked for leave, and his 'bowels could have been refreshed'. Was the love shown only to saints and outsiders? It is not unlikely. Unfortunately for Onesimus, he was not a saint and he was not an outsider. Was the love shown only to free men? Again, Onesimus was not a free man.

Thank God, who does not respect persons, for bringing salvation to the Jews as well as to the Gentiles. Until we ask ourselves pragmatic questions about this book of the Bible, we may never understand the truth. Why would a servant steal and run away from him, a man full of practical love? Had Philemon bought stock shares for Onesimus, I am sure he would never leave him. Had he been paying his or his children's school fees, I am sure he would never have absconded. Onesimus was a servant and treated as a servant. I still cannot figure out how any heart can withstand practical love. With a home of love, where else would a servant want to go? To whom do we go? Who else has the word of life? What was the difference between Paul and Philemon? At Rome, this servant met Paul, a prisoner of both man and God, he met a servant of the Lord, he met Paul. There was something different in Paul that melted Onesimus. Had Christianity repelled him, he would have been driven back at first sight. Was he just a bad man who would not repent despite the prayers of Philemon? No. He met Paul, and something practical about Christianity, something about a prisoner and a servant of the Lord, touched him. He changed. He met a servant in Paul and a master in Jesus. At that point, he understood Christianity and the gospel.

Where are we going with all this? The servant loved him. I am bold to say that Isaac earned it. The servant wanted the best for him. How easy it was for the servant to have plotted against Abraham and the son. No, he would not do that. Though when he prayed, he prayed to the 'God of his master, Abraham', and it is evident he also knew this God. How many Christian homes today teach their servants about the gospel? Oh! Like Philemon, our fame is shed abroad, but at home, we are masters to our servants. Isaac was living a plain life with the servants. No pride. As Paul would put it, 'He wasn't thinking of himself more highly' than is necessary. What do we see in our churches today? Servants are spotted with their shabby dresses in the church. Subordinates are treated like nobody. Christians do cruel things to their subordinates, mistreat them, and then ask them to be good. If your subordinates cannot, from an act of honour, work for you, you are not a good master. This is my submission.

Before you are ready for marriage, your spirit must be refined. Let us not deceive ourselves. Isaac was someone whom a servant or subordinate wished the best for. Let no pastor or teacher deceive you about marriage. How they preach we should pray and pray through and then God will show you your wife. Yet people have all commonly married people from homes they know, fellowships they worshipped in, or people they have known for a time. Some have even had one or two broken relationship after being 'led' by God. We exalt prayer more than necessary. We have forgotten that Eve did not go through character-moulding life-changing events and trials to become who she was. She was made to specification. These tests and trials of life mould us. We may not pray for test and trials, for indeed we do not know what we need. We must, however, renew our minds daily to make God the final authority in our lives.

Isaac was good to the extent that his subordinate would want the best for him. It takes sacrifice. It takes a humble lifestyle. It takes the right choice of words. It takes love and giving. Isaac was so nice to servants that he would consent to a servant making the decision of a lifetime for him. It takes trust. He was so kind to his subordinate that he could now trust him.

In those days in Nigeria, when most secondary schools were boarding schools, only a few seniors dared to send juniors to fetch drinking water for them. There were cases of juniors urinating inside the cups before serving the water, just to get back at the wicked seniors. Even then, there were juniors who would throng a particular senior as schoolchildren (servants), because such a senior was good and kind and would not by invoking seniority, eat their provisions or food ration. Until our spirits are good enough for our subordinates to want, of their own volition, to serve us in honour, we are not ready for marriage. This is especially needful for the man who believes he is the master of the house and the wife is the servant. We must love and honour our wives in such a way that they will only think of our interest. Love begets love. Trust begets trust. To achieve this feat may take a lifetime, but it takes the initial step of recognizing God and His word as the final authority in our lives. God seeks those who will worship Him in spirit and in truth.

1.4   Isaac: accepted father's and servant's decision

And the servant told Isaac all things that he had done. And Isaac brought her into his mother Sarah's tent, and took Rebekah, and she became his wife; and he loved her: and Isaac was comforted after his mother's death. (Gen. 24:66–67 KJV)

It is easy to overlook this value in this man. Perhaps this is the most important personality we must possess to be ready for a lasting relationship. The Spirit does not expressly state that Isaac was told about the plan. Judging from the verse above, he listened to the servant, he was satisfied, and then he took her immediately as a wife. We are bold to assume that he knew of the plan. Had he not known of it, he would have rebelled immediately. I think at a younger age, this man was willing to die as a sacrifice just for the fact that the father told him that God asked for him. I do not think he was not too young to defend himself. We can safely assume only two things: either the warrior in Abraham came out, overcame Isaac, and tied him up; or he simply, with tears but with a firm heart, talked Isaac into it. I suppose the former would have generated bitterness towards the father and towards God. The latter means that Isaac understood God, believed Him, and may have even encouraged his father to go ahead. It is easier for us to accept the latter. At any rate, here was a man some years later. He knew he was a miracle. He had literally died and resurrected. Like his servant, he must have known that God is able to provide. The servant was to go and find a wife. He was to trust God. Of course, God was with him. This may not have been an express instruction from God, but it was nonetheless in the will of God. All Isaac was to do was to sit and wait upon God. Isaac accepted his father's decision. The father had made several correct decisions in the past along the will of God and Isaac respected that.

In those days, in a culture I am familiar with in Nigeria, Africa (this was common with most other African cultures), most marriages were arranged by parents. People were even betrothed before they were born. People grew up and were introduced to their spouses. We may have heard of abuses of human rights with this method. We can boldly submit that this was far more successful than not. Maybe when we see a church or our fellowship centres being so strict about issues of marriage, we should know that it is because they have seen a lot. Some churches try to make sure they follow up every inch of the way. They even regulate visits and buying presents and gifts. It is wrong for anyone to condemn these acts by the church. The Church of Christ must protect her own. How do we explain a man who is HIV positive marrying in the church without letting at least the partner know of it? It is wrong to deceive your partner into marriage. Some churches would demand that medical testing be done before approving marriage. Let us be slow to speak in accusation of such churches. What are we saying here? When people who are our parents, leaders, pastors, teachers, and so forth, get involved in our choices of partners, let us not reject them outright, especially on issues that are not anti-Bible.

Isaac accepted his father's choice. The father knew his son was of God and wanted someone of God for him. Are we Christians at home? Do people know the values we hold so dearly? If our beliefs are not acknowledged at home, we may find out that our loved ones will make choices for us based on their own values. Most often, we have conflicts. Isaac was known at home. The servant did not express surprise to find him praying in the field when he returned. Do our fathers know we are Christians? Do they know we do not smoke? Do they know we do not drink alcohol? Do we keep quiet when we are supposed to let people know our values? Are we waiting until the wedding day to let them know, for instance, that our partners do not drink alcohol? Will they be surprised that day? What types of clothes will our parents buy for us? Before our parents can make decisions for us, especially life-threatening ones, we must be known as Christians at home. Let us declare who we are at home. Permit me to include *everywhere* as well. Let it be that our bosses know what we can do and what we cannot do. Let all know where we stand. It is only then that people will be able to make the right decisions for us. In fact, it is my submission that if nobody, including family and friends, can recommend spouses for us; it is a sign of inconsistency and instability. Worse still is if the one we have chosen does not match the image of the spouse that our loved ones would have recommended for us.

Isaac honoured his father because it was a terrain that the father had walked and understood well. It was a path that Isaac had taken or planned to take. His father knew it and gave biblical support. Who would not appreciate the decisions or advice of a man like Eliezer, who always worshipped Him and was in constant tune with Him?

Let people know who we are and what we believe in; when they then help us make decisions, they will always be positive to our overall goals. Then, and only then, will we be able to respect their decisions about us. Whatever we believe in, whether good or bad, we must let everyone know where we stand on issues.

1.5 Isaac: readiness and timing

Isaac was forty years old when he married Rebekah.

> And Isaac was forty years old when he took Rebekah to wife, the daughter of Bethuel the Syrian of Padanaram, the sister to Laban the Syrian. (Gen. 25:20 KJV)

There was this timing and readiness for marriage. While there is no cast-iron rule about this, we would all frown at a twelve-year-old boy insisting on marriage. At least we still have an age where adulthood begins. Who knows what will happen in the next generation? On the other hand some indeed are not interested in marriage. If there was any man who was a miracle, it was Isaac. Oh, how some people believe that they are specially loved by God. In this confidence, Isaac could have gone ahead with the marriage. He was born miraculously. He had a warrior as a father. The father had men of war among his servants. Do we not think he could have just sent them to check out the neighbourhood and get the most beautiful wife? He knew marriage was not like that. Do we say he knew from experience?

Isaac had a rich man as a father. Could Abraham not have organized a beauty contest as the king did for Queen Esther? Could he not have done all this before Isaac was forty? Thank God he had a patient father. Who could be more patient than a man who waited for a child for about one hundred years? It took three years after the death of Sarah before they decided to find a wife for him.

> *Then Abraham fell upon his face, and laughed, and said in his heart, Shall a child be born unto him that is an hundred years old? and shall Sarah, that is ninety years old, bear?* (Gen. 17:17 KJV)

> *And Sarah was an hundred and seven and twenty years old: these were the years of the life of Sarah.* (Gen. 23:1 KJV)

> *And Isaac was forty years old when he took Rebekah to wife, the daughter of Bethuel the Syrian of Padanaram, the sister to Laban the Syrian.* (Gen 25:20 KJV)

They took their time. Isaac had a prayer warrior as a father. Abraham was the first recorded saint to bargain with God. Even this would not make Isaac marry until he was forty. Could this man who in prayer saw God not have hastened things up with prayer, as some believe today? They forget that God has his own timetable. They forget that God sees the overall plan. What else can we say? Isaac had the fellowship of a worshipper as a servant. The servant was very practical as well. All this would wait until the man was ready. How was the man ready?

It seems to me that until there was an obvious vacuum in the young man's life by the death of the mother, marriage was not well timed. Does this not follow the example of Adam? The Bible says that Isaac was comforted after he married Rebekah.

> *And Isaac brought her into his mother Sarah's tent, and took Rebekah, and she became his wife; and he loved her: and Isaac was comforted after his mother's death.* (Gen. 24:67 KJV)

When did he lose the comfort? Was he not comforted when the mother was alive? This period of loss brought lack of comfort. In the midst of people, permit me to say men of God, in the fellowship of worshippers, he was alone and needed 'help meet for him'. There are some parents that pressure their children to marry on the excuse that they are the only children or that they need an opposite sex in the home. If there was a man who needed grandchildren quickly, we could say it was Abraham. He was 140 years old. God promised him that he would become a father of nations. Isaac was a child of promise. Is it not as if Abraham waited until he was sure Isaac needed a wife rather than him (Abraham) needing a wife for his son? Abraham waited until he was sure he was not helping God as many people do today? They forget the lesson of Uzzah, when he helped God to hold the ark of covenant. Do we think God would have let his ark of covenant fall to the ground?

We may not be able to fix any age or even age boundary. Let us conclude this way.

> *And Isaac brought her into his mother Sarah's tent . . .* (Gen. 24:67 KJV)

Is there a tent for you and your partner? Can you maintain that tent? Then you are ready to take a partner. Even at then, we should not forget that some are born rich, others achieve it, and some may never be rich. If we are born rich, all is well and good, and like Isaac, we should move into our parents' tents. If we are not born rich and we have to achieve it, please let us take our time. The Bible says a man that cannot take care of his house is worse than an infidel:

> *But if any provide not for his own, and specially for those of his own house, he hath denied the faith, and is worse than an infidel.* (1 Tim. 5:8 KJV)

We need to be able to provide food, health, and protection inside our tents. To fend for our tents, we need to have stable sources of income for them. It does not matter from which side it is coming, whether from the woman or from the man. To fend for our tents, we need trades or jobs that bring in income. Until there is a tent that can be comfortable and the comfort can be maintained, it is not yet time to marry.

1.6 Isaac: a man who walked with God, a man of prayer

And Isaac went out to meditate in the field at the eventide: and he lifted up his eyes, and saw, and, behold, the camels were coming. (Gen. 24:63 KJV)

And Isaac entreated the LORD for his wife, because she was barren: and the LORD was entreated of him, and Rebekah his wife conceived. (Gen. 25:21 KJV)

And after that came his brother out, and his hand took hold on Esau's heel; and his name was called Jacob: and Isaac was threescore years old when she bare them. (Gen. 25:26 KJV)

These few verses give us an insight into the life of Isaac. For one, he knew where to go when there was a hard decision to make. When life dishes out its bitter pills for us to swallow, we must trust God. The journey by the servant Eliezer may have taken several days. Isaac went to meditate and then lifted up his eyes and, surprisingly, saw camels coming. Something was shaking him up to his marrows but he knew what to do. Again, after nineteen years of marriage, there was no child. He went again and prayed, and the Lord answered him. Life is extremely uncertain. Do we really expect less?

The Bible says in Ecclesiastes that life can be extremely uncertain.

I returned, and saw under the sun, that the race is not to the swift, nor the battle to the strong, neither yet bread to the wise, nor yet riches to men of understanding, nor yet favour to men of skill; but time and chance happeneth to them all. For man also knoweth not his time: as the fishes that are taken in an evil net, and as the birds that are caught in the snare; so are the sons of men snared in an evil time, when it falleth suddenly upon them.

This wisdom have I seen also under the sun, and it seemed great unto me: There was a little city, and few men within it; and there came a great king against it, and besieged it, and built great bulwarks against it: Now there was found in it a poor wise man, and he by his wisdom delivered the city; yet no man remembered that same poor man. Then said I, Wisdom is better than strength: nevertheless the poor man's wisdom is despised, and his words are not heard. The words of wise men are heard in quiet more than the cry of him that ruleth among fools. Wisdom is better than weapons of war: but one sinner destroyeth much good. (Eccles. 9:11-18 KJV)

In other words, we need to accept the following:

- That you are the swiftest does not mean you will win the race.
- That you are stronger than your opponent does not mean you will defeat him.
- That you are wise does not guarantee bread.
- That you are intelligent and have the best results does not mean you will eventually be richer than all your classmates.
- That you know the job does not always mean you will have favour and promotion.
- That being careful alone does not make you know when you are going to die.
- That poor people are not always appreciated despite their great feats.
- That the wisdom and words of the poor are despised.
- That fools will still reject your wise words.
- That wisdom is better than weapons of war in these days of war everywhere.
- That one loose sinner can wreck havoc and destroy much good.

Having considered all these, where is our strength? Where is our hope? I ask one disturbing question: was it Job's fault those calamities fell on him in the book of Job? Yet powers above, which in truth control everything in this world, discussed his case, as it were, in a cocktail party and decided to use his bitterness as a point to settle their arguments. I am tempted to believe they were capable of simulating the situation without involving the specimen. What can we say? He moves in mysterious ways, his wonders to perform.

Brothers and sisters, we stand only at the shadows of His mercies. Our hope in life should be built on nothing else than Jesus' blood and righteousness. Time and chance happen to us all. He is the one in control of time. Jesus said to his disciples,

> *And he said unto them, It is not for you to know the times or the seasons, which the Father hath put in his own power.* (Acts 1:7 KJV)

He actually rebuked the disciples. The Bible speaks about if the righteous scarcely be saved, what is the lot of the unsaved?

When we have realized that there is no hope other than Jesus, then we are ready for marriage. Do we have testimony of salvation? Abraham summed up this way.

> *The LORD God of heaven, which took me from my father's house, and from the land of my kindred, and which spake unto me, and that sware unto me, saying, Unto thy seed will I give this land; he shall send his angel before thee, and thou shalt take a wife unto my son from thence. And if the woman will not be willing to follow thee, then thou shalt be clear from this my oath: only bring not my son thither again.* (Gen. 24:7–8 KJV)

If the Lord has taken us, spoken to us, and sworn to us before now, we will be able to trust Him in the future.

Do we still depend on how smart we are like Jacob: planning, cheating, and running away? Until the Lord then break our thighs and make us realize that we cannot run any more from Esau (our past mistakes and failures), we will not hold unto the Lord to say, 'Bless me or I will not let you go.' Is walking with the Lord not simple—reading the Bible and applying it to our lives? The Bible is God speaking to us today. Let us depend on him. Was Hannah not right when she said, 'For by strength shall no man prevail'? We need God not just for marriage but also for life.

Let us use this time to explain the place of prayer in our lives and in finding a marriage partner. When you pray to God that you need a spouse, God will answer in any of several ways. He may send a vision giving specifics about your spouse. He may send an angel to give you instructions. He may send someone to introduce somebody to you. He may arrange circumstances and then you meet each other. Of course, when you meet the person, you begin to ask yourself, *Are you the one that is to come, or do I wait for another?* If God has sent an angel to you or has given you a vision, you go ahead and let the person in question know about your vision. If someone introduces somebody to you or you meet someone, then of course you pray for the Lord to lead you.

Now, whether vision, dreams, or just noticing someone, we all need to base our judgements on biblical values. No two wills of God will ever clash. The essence is, if I marry this person, I am not going to miss heaven; I am not going to displease God or live for God less; I am not going to drift in the secular world; and so on. These assessments may take weeks or even years. This is the courtship period. Once you have found out that you are on the right path, you can go ahead and marry. Of course, if you are on the wrong path, break it off! During this time, you will need to depend entirely on God, should you be making a mistake. Samuel made the wrong choice of a king six times. This man had started to hear from God at a tender age and literally lived in the presence of God. A man of God is not infallible. This is where we need prayer; to unravel things (character or personality) that will increase our faith or erode it in the plans to marry. No matter who you are or how you started the relationship, you need the angel of the Lord to always go before you, as in the story we have been considering.

1.7   Rebekah: a domestic sister

It is amazing what truth is in the Holy Scripture. How I pray that the Lord will help me to read the word more and more. As we stare into this perfect law of liberty, we discover certain truths.

Let us start with the fact that she was quite homely. The well of water was outside the city—not outside her compound. So do we want to assume that her house was the first house inside the city, which will just reduce the distance? What if we assume that her house was at the opposite end of the city? What we know of the distance is that a fit person could run it.

> And the damsel ran, and told them of her mother's house these things.
> And Rebekah had a brother, and his name was Laban: and Laban
> ran out unto the man, unto the well. (Gen. 24:28-29 KJV)

Rebekah ran and Laban ran. Let us pause and think of our moods the few times we had to do real manual labour. Do we remember how exactly we felt? She saw it as a household task that she must fulfil. She was not discouraged by the power involved. After fetching water for camels, she still had enough motivation to run. How many of us today complain of headaches after just walking? Let me add here that we are not against those who are medically unfit. The Lord will remember you and heal you in the name of Jesus. We are talking about laziness. How hard-working are we? Who sweeps/vacuums the house? When was the last time we scrubbed the bath in a good mood? When did we last a complete meal? Have we taken time to clean and polish our shoes recently? When did we last clean out the fridge in a good mood? I have seen sisters turning their bed sheets over when one side is dirty. Rebekah went outside the city gate to fetch water as a normal daily chore. This was the beginning of her meeting with Isaac.

Now let us look at the next fact:

> And he made his camels to kneel down without the city by a well of
> water at the time of the evening, even the time that women go out to
> draw water. (Gen. 24:11 KJV)

It was the proper time. It was the appointed time. It was the right time. What are we saying? It was the normal time when people fetch water. Have we ever burnt food because we were watching TV? Have we not been late—even for a church appointment—because we were talking with a friend? It was evening, it was time to fetch water, and

Rebekah was there, actively fetching water. We all need to learn from this: doing the right thing at the right time. We tend to leave all our clothes dirty for days until we have exhausted the clean ones. We wait until we are expecting a visitor before we clean the house. We wait until exam time to read our textbooks. We know many people whose anointing had been downplayed because of their character. Someone once said, 'When God lifts a man up, even in the area of marriage, it is character that will sustain him.' Why do you think the Holy Scripture spent so much time on 'thou shalt' and 'thou shalt not'? It is because God wants us to follow rules, thereby subjecting the flesh.

The next fact: is the most interesting if not the most important characteristic needed to find a partner and to keep one. A teenager once asked me at a teen retreat whether it was right for one to have a member of the opposite sex as one's best friend. I answered that it will almost lead to sin, except when we are talking about engaged or married people. Rebekah associated with womanhood. She was proud of her sex. She was proud to be a woman. Why did she not go before the women's time? As a woman herself, Rebekah like the women in her days. Until, in the church of Christ, sisters act as sisters in submission and brothers equally act as brothers in love, we may find out that broken courtship and divorces will unfortunately continue to exist. Let us take our proper places. If you are a woman, be a woman (whatever that means!). If you are a man, be a man and have enough strength to move furniture around or push a broken car out of harm's way. Rebekah went out when women went out. This again can be viewed in terms of responsibility. She ought to be out; she was out. How responsible are we in the house of God today? Do we fulfil our roles? Can people count on us to get things done?

> *Therefore to him that knoweth to do good, and doeth it not, to him it is sin.* (James 4:17 KJV)

Until we stand and fulfil our roles (not only at home), we may find that we are not building the right foundation for our homes. Until then, no matter how much prayer is going on inside the church for marriage, we may never be able to show examples of how good homes should be.

In expanding on responsibility, the Bible says:

> *And it came to pass, before he had done speaking, that, behold,*
> *Rebekah came out, who was born to Bethuel, son of Milcah, the wife*
> *of Nahor, Abraham's brother, with her pitcher upon her shoulder.*
> (Gen. 24:15 KJV)

The water jar was on her shoulder. It was business time. It was time
to be serious. It was (and even now it is) customary for women to
carry water jars on their shoulders. Rebekah knew it was business
time, and she was up for it. Have we not met some people that we
think are clowns, but when seriousness is demanded, they are dead
serious? Have we not heard of 'shouldering one's responsibility'?
Rebekah faced it. It was the way to fetch water, and she did it that
way. No shortcut. We should covet this noble spirit before marriage,
taking up responsibility and facing it squarely. This one virtue can
single-handedly keep a home.

1.8   Rebekah: physically fit

> *And the damsel was very fair to look upon, a virgin, neither had*
> *any man known her: and she went down to the well, and filled her*
> *pitcher, and came up.* (Gen. 24:16 KJV)

> *And Jesus increased in . . . stature . . .* (Luke 2:52 KJV)

At first glance, we may think beauty is natural, and as such, we cannot
do anything about it. I want to believe that while some are born
beautiful (and mind you, they can lose those looks), others can make
themselves beautiful. We shall attempt to look at several things that
can make one fair to look upon.

Let us start with the skin. It does not matter whether our skin is
red, yellow, black, or white—what matters is whether we are taking
care of it. Do we know certain body creams that our skins are
sensitive to? Do we avoid unnecessarily hurting or bruising our
skin? How about our hair, our moustache, our beards? Do we tidy
them up? For our sisters, are we taking care of our eyelashes and

our eyebrows? Are we taking care of our teeth? How many times have we have seen sisters dress so shabbily that we do not want to associate with them? Clothing does not need to be expensive but it needs to be neat and well ironed. How dare we say we are praying for a husband and then our hair smells and our clothes are dirty with missing buttons? We should be attractive. Use the right perfume or deodorant. Let us make sure that anyone who sees us sees neatness.

For men, what right have we to start praying for a woman we want to care for when we cannot take care of our beards and moustaches? How can we say that we do not have time for our facial hair and then want to have time for another full human being? Attend to your facial hair. Use aftershave. Use cologne. Get your clothes neat and manly. Do we not wonder when we see men's shoes unpolished? Think about the fingernails and the toenails. Let us stay neat and well kept, and then we will see people around us giving the right signals. Rebekah dressed well, and then she fit into prayer.

Again talking about physical fitness, Rebekah was fit.

> And it came to pass, before he had done speaking, that, behold, Rebekah came out, who was born to Bethuel, son of Milcah, the wife of Nahor, Abraham's brother, with her pitcher upon her shoulder. And the damsel was very fair to look upon, a virgin, neither had any man known her: and she went down to the well, and filled her pitcher, and came up. And the servant ran to meet her, and said, Let me, I pray thee, drink a little water of thy pitcher. And she said, Drink, my lord: and she hasted, and let down her pitcher upon her hand, and gave him drink. And when she had done giving him drink, she said, I will draw water for thy camels also, until they have done drinking. And she hasted, and emptied her pitcher into the trough, and ran again unto the well to draw water, and drew for all his camels. And the man wondering at her held his peace, to wit whether the LORD had made his journey prosperous or not. And it came to pass, as the camels had done drinking, that the man took a golden earring of half a shekel weight, and two bracelets for her hands of ten shekels weight of gold; And said, Whose daughter art thou?

> *tell me, I pray thee: is there room in thy father's house for us*
> *in? And she said unto him, I am the daughter of Bethuel th⁞*
> *Milcah, which she bare unto Nahor. She said moreover un⁞*
> *We have both straw and provender enough, and room to lo⁞*
> *And the man bowed down his head, and worshipped the L⁞*
> *And he said, Blessed be the LORD God of my master Ab⁞*
> *who hath not left destitute my master of his mercy and his t⁞*
> *being in the way, the LORD led me to the house of my m⁞*
> *brethren. And the damsel ran, and told them of her mother's⁞*
> *these things.* (Gen. 24:15-28 KJV).

She walked so briskly that she literally appeared before ⁞
could finish speaking. She went down to the well (slop⁞
water, and off she went vigorously. It took the servant to r⁞
up with her who was just walking. She let down her jar ⁞
for the servant and ran to fetch water for the camels an⁞
with the servant. Then she ran home. Are we getting the g⁞
I will repeat that we are not talking about those who are ⁞
unfit. We are saying that some people just laze about, and ⁞
they are unfit. Men are generally assumed to be more pow⁞
women. A sister will leave you if you need help climbing ⁞
and it is not a medical condition. What are you doing about ⁞
if you have it? Are you watching your weight? Do you wa⁞
you eat? When married, we will need strength for our ⁞
What are we going to do then? Why do we not resume t⁞
class? Why do we not resume that jogging and swimming ⁞
used to do? Physical fitness is needed during wedding prep⁞
wedding ceremonies, sexual intercourse, childbearing, and ⁞
Rebekah was fit. She fetched water for camels to drink. Car⁞
known to be one of the greatest consumers of water at one ⁞
The Bible says ten camels. She fetched water for the servant a⁞
men with him, and then she still had enough power to run ⁞
How many of us today can run? Some of us are so sluggis⁞
so slow. We cannot get things done because we are lazy. So ⁞
happens? The partner comes around, sees us, and turns away. ⁞
cannot change this. In fact, prayer does not make us fit. We h⁞
make ourselves fit.

ıother point we need to talk about here is in the verse below.

> *And the damsel was very fair to look upon, a virgin, neither had any man known her: and she went down to the well, and filled her pitcher, and came up.* (Gen. 24:16 KJV)

he Bible says she was a virgin. We can view this in two ways. Either ıe was physically a virgin or she dressed up as one. In development f spirit, these are both important. She dressed up as a virgin. By so ɔing, she gave the right signals to all around. Why should we wear wedding ring or an engagement ring when we know nothing is appening? Some men are always with some sisters that no other ıen would want to go near. In my culture, married people dress ı a particular way. Why should you as a single person dress up as married person? Join the right circle where you can get married. Though Rebekah came up when women came up to fetch water, he was identified as a virgin. If we want to get married, let us display ɔurselves that way.

Then of course, we can also say that she was a virgin. What a hard virtue to find these days. This has to do with how we condition our minds. What do we watch? What do we hear? How much do we guard our minds jealously? To find a virgin if Jesus were to be born today would have taken God a lot of effort, especially in our modern world. Using the words of Jesus, 'from the beginning', it was meant to be one man and one wife together until death do them part. God instructed the high priests to marry only virgins. If you are still one as a man or as a woman, please guard it fiercely. It is a sign of good things to come.

1.9 Rebekah: skillful sister

> *And she went down to the well, and filled her pitcher, and came up.* (Gen. 24:16 KJV)

> *She lighted off the camel.* (Gen. 24:64 KJV)

We would be making a mistake if we assumed that fetching water from the well was like fetching water from the kitchen sink. From what we have seen in films, magazines, and pictures, we understand that special skills were needed to fetch water from the well. Rebekah had the skill to get water out of that well with speed. In those days, it was easy to find a family where women depended entirely on the man's income. Now, with economic realities, it is ill advised for one to suggest that women should always sit back in the man's tent doing nothing. They should acquire skills. No knowledge, they say, is lost. Do you know how to use a typewriter? Do you have basic computer knowledge? Do you know how to use some modern machines: washing machines, clothes dryers, sewing machines, and so forth? It is important to learn skills that may eventually put bread on our tables. It is equally important to learn some other skills as well. Learn how to change burnt bulbs, paint, arrange flowers, and change flat tyres. Learn new languages. Just learn what you can learn. You never know when you may need new skills. These are values that your partner, your wife or husband, will find attractive about you. It is like icing on the cake.

1.10   Rebekah: a helping sister

And let it come to pass, that the damsel to whom I shall say, Let down thy pitcher, I pray thee, that I may drink; and she shall say, Drink, and I will give thy camels drink also: let the same be she that thou hast appointed for thy servant Isaac; and thereby shall I know that thou hast shewed kindness unto my master. (Gen. 24:14 KJV)

I am bold to submit that even if you line up thousands of women to be tested with this prayer, only Rebekah and people like her will pass the test. This prayer was directed at the heart, not actions. Indeed, God assesses our actions.

Talk no more so exceeding proudly; let not arrogancy come out of your mouth: for the LORD is a God of knowledge, and by him actions are weighed. (1 Sam. 2:3 KJV)

In these days of kidnappers, rapists, and thieves, we often advise others not only to keep from talking to strangers but also not to listen to them. The servants desired just to talk to someone. Do we take time to listen to strangers even when we know we are safe? Are we patient enough? Rebekah's flow of thought was disturbed. Her peace and privacy were invaded. What would we feel when a complete stranger who has been standing by runs up to us suddenly? Do we think she was not embarrassed? How many of us wait to hear the answer when we ask colleagues how they are? In our modern world, with all its dangers, we may tell our children and youths not to entertain strangers. However, the problem is, we grow up with this mindset, and even when we are old and protected, we may never be able to strike a balance. God will help us.

The next thing is that she was to answer this stranger as part of answer to the prayer made above. Eliezer needed an answer, not snubbing. Have you ever needed an answer and then been ignored? The important thing here is not whether she refused or granted the request. The important thing is that she answered. Let us pause and think about something. Have we not been asked of something before, and all we did was look at the person asking and then quietly, without a word, grant the request and then leave? Had Rebekah behaved that way, she would have failed the test. Does that make sense?

She answered 'Drink, my lord' and then with haste brought down her water jar. In a public place, she gave these noble words. Are we surprised that this woman took the place of Sarah to comfort Isaac? Was this not a family tradition? Sarah called her husband lord. Here we have Rebekah calling even a servant lord. This may be equivalent to 'It is my pleasure, sir'. She let down her jar in haste. Let us watch our language in the church today. Actions, they say, speak louder than words. Her actions were purely her intentions. Jesus says that out of the belly comes all evil thoughts. We have cases where we have asked for something, and before we were given, we declined because of the way it was being offered to us. Rebekah gave with all her heart. This is what Paul considered cheerful giving.

Rebekah saw men and animals in need:

> *And the man came into the house: and he ungirded his camels, and gave straw and provender for the camels, and water to wash his feet, and the men's feet that were with him.* (Gen. 24:32 KJV)

She responded immediately. The book of James, the brother of Jesus, puts it this way:

> *Pure religion and undefiled before God and the Father is this, To visit the fatherless and widows in their affliction, and to keep himself unspotted from the world.* (James 1:27 KJV)

Jesus Himself puts it this way:

> *Then shall the King say unto them on his right hand, Come, ye blessed of my Father, inherit the kingdom prepared for you from the foundation of the world: For I was an hungered, and ye gave me meat: I was thirsty, and ye gave me drink: I was a stranger, and ye took me in: Naked, and ye clothed me: I was sick, and ye visited me: I was in prison, and ye came unto me. Then shall the righteous answer him, saying, Lord, when saw we thee an hungered, and fed thee? or thirsty, and gave thee drink? When saw we thee a stranger, and took thee in? or naked, and clothed thee? Or when saw we thee sick, or in prison, and came unto thee? And the King shall answer and say unto them, Verily I say unto you, Inasmuch as ye have done it unto one of the least of these my brethren, ye have done it unto me.* (Matt. 25:34-40 KJV)

When Eliezer set out to look for a wife, he was out to look for someone who was to inherit Abraham's riches, someone who was going to be his boss. The only person qualified would be the person whose heart was not raised by an abundance of wealth. In truth it does not profit a man to gain the whole world and lose his soul. Agur prayed:

> *Two things have I required of thee; deny me them not before I die: Remove far from me vanity and lies: give me neither poverty nor riches; feed me with food convenient for me: Lest I be full, and deny*

thee, and say, Who is the LORD? or lest I be poor, and steal, and take the name of my God in vain. (Prov. 30:7-9)

This prayer may be selfish and lack responsibility, but we cannot overlook the sincerity. Paul said we have our reward:

Not that I speak in respect of want: for I have learned, in whatsoever state I am, therewith to be content. I know both how to be abased, and I know how to abound: every where and in all things I am instructed both to be full and to be hungry, both to abound and to suffer need. (Phil. 4:11-12 KJV)

Rebekah would have riches yet would not deny God. In the choice of this woman, the servant needed someone detached from this world and looking unto heaven for a new city 'whose builder and maker is God'. She must be someone who would store up treasures in heaven, where moths and thieves cannot make contact. Had God not warned that we should not forget the poor (for there will always be poor in Israel). Rebekah was going to be catapulted from nothing to glory. She must not be attached to glamour and vanity. She must see everything as from God and use it to help the work of God. She must not come into the house of Abraham and turn herself into a mean queen. Again, I feel that even if there were a thousand women in the city, with this prayer of the servant, only people like Rebekah would have passed the test. Today, how do people pray? 'God, the first man to come to church today is the man you have chosen.' How dare we pray this way and not be confused. Are there not real disciples who would be telling the beggar by the gate, 'Silver and gold we do not have . . .' and then come into the church late? We are not saying here that signs in prayer are wrong. What we are saying is that the prayer of this servant was directed at the heart, not just action. It was for the spirit.

In addition, Rebekah noticed the men with the servant and the animals. How many of us actually take note of our surroundings, let alone the animals? Many of us would have failed this test! The servant prayed this 'dangerous' prayer, that the woman would notice the men and the camels and know they needed water. Rebekah was to be a friend of animals. She was to help animals. Was this spirit not very important, especially for a woman who was going to be married to a shepherd? How many of us would have failed this test outright? Rebekah saw the camels and noticed they needed water. How alert are we to our surroundings? Some people are so meticulous that if another person touches their clothes in their wardrobe, they will know. Some can tell when another man has entered his office. Let us be aware of our surroundings. It sure helps.

Rebekah was asked for water; she gave also to the camels. She was asked for a room, and she gave to the camels as well, along with feed for the animals. She was caring and easy-going. She was a brother's keeper. If she meant to help you, she would help you to the last. She was a true daughter of God who is able to 'do exceeding abundantly above' all that we ask or think. Paul, in his letter to Timothy, summed it up this way:

> *Charge them that are rich in this world, that they be not highminded, nor trust in uncertain riches, but in the living God, who giveth us richly all things to enjoy; That they do good, that they be rich in good works, ready to distribute, willing to communicate; Laying up in store for themselves a good foundation against the time to come, that they may lay hold on eternal life.* (1 Tim. 6:17-19 KJV)

Rebekah was going to be rich; the servant needed someone who could do good and be rich in good deeds—a woman who was willing to share. Rebekah was ready to share even her home with strangers. She was not like Laban. The Bible says that when he saw 'the ring and the bracelets on his sister's wrist', then he heard the story. Do we do good only to those who can repay? Jesus said we have our reward.

The conclusion is that when we are ready to marry, we must be prepared to help. Helping minds will assist us in living with our spouses. It will help us to do certain things without expecting a thank you. It will make us appreciate help when we receive it from others.

1.11   Rebekah: the submissive sister

And the damsel ran, and told them of her mother's house these things.
(Gen. 24:28 KJV)

As part of the signs for the last days, the Bible says children shall be disrespectful to parents. Let us investigate how serious this is in the Holy Scriptures.

If a woman also vow a vow unto the LORD, and bind herself by a bond, being in her father's house in her youth; And her father hear her vow, and her bond wherewith she hath bound her soul, and her father shall hold his peace at her: then all her vows shall stand, and every bond wherewith she hath bound her soul shall stand. But if her father disallow her in the day that he heareth; not any of her vows, or of her bonds wherewith she hath bound her soul, shall stand: and the LORD shall forgive her, because her father disallowed her. (Num. 30:3-4 KJV)

The Lord makes it clear here that He respects the authority He has placed over us. Vows to the Lord could be considered annulled by the Lord when the authority over us rejects such vows. Paul admonished us all to obey all authorities.

Let every soul be subject unto the higher powers. For there is no power but of God: the powers that be are ordained of God. Whosoever therefore resisteth the power, resisteth the ordinance of God: and they that resist shall receive to themselves damnation. For rulers are not a terror to good works, but to the evil. Wilt thou then not be afraid of the power? do that which is good, and thou shalt have praise of the same: For he is the minister of God to thee for good. But if thou do that which is evil, be afraid; for he beareth not the sword in vain: for he is the minister of God, a revenger to execute wrath upon him that doeth evil. Wherefore ye must needs be subject, not only for wrath, but also for conscience sake. For this cause pay ye tribute also: for they are God's ministers, attending continually upon this very thing.
(Rom. 13:1-6 KJV)

Once Rebekah started hearing things—lovely things, for that matter—and her heart was beginning to be swayed, she went to the authority over her. Do we really believe in the church authority? Let me make it clear here that if we break any law of the church in the process of coming together with our spouses, we should pray for forgiveness. It is the church. It is the power over us. If you do not like the laws, talk about it or leave the church. Some churches believe that before the man ever speaks to the woman, he should let the marriage committee know. Others believe you may go ahead and speak to her as a man and thereafter come to the church after the woman had agreed to marry you. Whatever the laws of the church are, let us be careful not to disobey. Apart from church, of course, we have parental authority. As I said earlier, if we declare who we are at home, our parents will not be surprised when we bring someone to them. Let us allow our parents to know who we are. Arguments about our beliefs and convictions should be well known before we marry. If, for example, our parents do not like a particular race, why wait until we bring someone from that race home to start the war?

Rebekah's household did all the negotiations, all the talking. They asked the tough questions. I cannot say how much we involve the church and our parents. All I know is that once men and brethren have known you well, they will always be interested in your well-being. We will know who wants our good. Allow them to ask the real questions and make the necessary enquiries. In my culture, 'spies' are sent by parents to investigate the other side, asking questions about hereditary illnesses, demonic influences, and the like. This is good. Rebekah allowed the authority over her to be involved and ask the relevant questions.

What if our parents just continue to dwell on things that are not relevant to happiness of the home and godliness of the union? Rebekah had the last say. I cannot say here where we should strike the balance. This is where we need the counsel of the church. Maybe we should just wait and pray. Maybe we should go ahead and be careless of the consequences. All of this depends on the particular situation. One cannot generalize this case. Just be led by God and by His prophets. We have biblical values. Let those guide us. If, for example, they want us to marry unbelievers, we know what the Bible says. Let me repeat that more often than not, that if we keep letting people know who we are and what we believe in, they will have already formed an opinion about us. There will not be a fight.

In conclusion, if the people, who have been with us for years, maybe twenty years, maybe thirty years, are suddenly thrown away because we want to marry a stranger, woe betides that stranger. How can we disregard our loved ones' feelings, the bound of friendship, and marry someone we have just met? How could a stranger to a person's life allow the person to throw away his or her parents and friends because of their new relationship? And that stranger will be hoping not to be thrown away with time too, by another desire of his spouse. If our spouses have been standing their grounds, boundaries would have been settled before we met them. One good sign of a spouse is one who has long-time friends. If you are good, friends and foes will say that you are good. The difference is that some will be happy with it, and others will hate you for it.

1.12 Joseph and Mary: an example of an engaged and married couple

The Bible did not speak so much about their parents or who sanctioned the marriage contract. Maybe it was not so important in the storyline, so as usual, the Spirit was silent over it. This is a lesson we should learn in everyday talking and storytelling. Is this not what is meant by James when he said we should be slow to speak? In essence, let us be careful when we talk.

> *Wherefore, my beloved brethren, let every man be swift to hear, slow to speak, slow to wrath.* (James 1:19 KJV)

It helps us to be sure of what we mean to say. Once out, words can never be revoked. The book of Proverbs sums it up; it says to stay out of trouble by minding what you say.

> *Whoso keepeth his mouth and his tongue keepeth his soul from troubles.* (Prov. 21:23 KJV)

The story says they were engaged to each other. Using the Bible language, they were betrothed to each other. This is to promise 'by one's truth'. From the time of betrothal, the woman was regarded as the lawful wife of the man to whom she was betrothed (Deut. 28:30; Judg. 14:2, 8; Matt. 1:18-21). So the laws of Moses bound them. Let us look at the laws.

> *If a damsel that is a virgin be betrothed unto an husband, and a man find her in the city, and lie with her; Then ye shall bring them both out unto the gate of that city, and ye shall stone them with stones that they die; the damsel, because she cried not, being in the city; and the man, because he hath humbled his neighbour's wife: so thou shalt put away evil from among you. But if a man find a betrothed damsel in the field, and the man force her, and lie with her: then the man only that lay with her shall die: But unto the damsel thou shalt do nothing; there is in the damsel no sin worthy of death: for as when a man riseth against his neighbour, and slayeth him, even so is this matter: For he found her in the field, and the betrothed damsel cried, and there was none to save her.* (Deut. 22:23-27 KJV)

The angel appeared to Mary to announce the birth of our Lord Jesus, and Mary asked, 'How shall this be, seeing that I know not a man?' Mary was wondering how this could be when she was a virgin. Besides, if you are an angel from the Lord, you must know the scriptures. If I am found not to be a virgin, I should die. If I say I was raped, I should die because I should have cried out that same day, to say the least. She may have also wondered of Joseph accepting responsibility which will not only be a shame to a just man, but also make him a liar. Mary was wondering how to reconcile this news with the scriptures. The Bible admonishes us to rightly divide the word of truth. If only people in pastoral schools had tried to reconcile all their 'God spoke to me', all their visions and dreams, with the written word. If only a lot of our pastors and church leaders profess that though we or an angel from heaven preach any other gospel unto the church than that which we have received, such should be 'accursed'. Mary insisted on reconciling annunciation with what the holy word was saying. Two wills of God cannot clash. How can God tell you to marry a woman who will come and lead you to dishonour your father and mother?

How can the Lord lead you so you can no longer take care of your home as a pastor? Is it not ridiculous how a lot of us are lead by God to disobey the known word? You need to hear brethren claiming of being led by God. We must query even angelic messages with the unchanging word of God. Some are even afraid to query their pastors, all in the name of man of God. I do not preach rebellion. No, not at all. I am only saying that as Christians, if we must remain in this race, grounded and settled and be not moved with every wind of doctrine, we need to be able to query our dreams and visions and even our pastor and our 'angels' with the written word of God. Only then will we be able to arrest the wind of divorce, shame of wrangling among pastors, and such things in the church today.

It is interesting to note here that the angel who 'stands before the lord' and who smote Zacharias with dumbness took time to explain things to Mary. Zacharias reacted differently. He was like, 'Give me a sign so I can be sure of this vision. I am already old.' He needed a sign because he felt this news was not true. He was old and his wife was too. The angel noted that he did not believe him. This annoyed the angel, and the angel ran a quick CV of himself for Zacharias and then gave him one serious sign. Mary, on the other hand, felt this was true, but death looms around a woman without a husband found with a child. The angel even gave a physical sign to her, telling her that her cousin Elizabeth was pregnant right then. Who says we cannot question men of God with the scriptures? Who says we cannot question even God with his word. He says to bring forth your reasons. This is what I think Moses did when he interceded for the people of Israel, while he prayed and reminded God that loving and merciful God should not just wipe out a people for his namesake. What I also think this was what happened when Zedekiah reminded God of how he has been good and followed the laws of God. God has given us the word. No other vision should work against it. Any vision or dream that does not align itself with the scriptures should be disregarded and avoided like a plague. The scripture is not only to be claimed for prosperity and healing as some preach today or make it seem, it is the guideline of life. Stick to it during courtship and after marriage. Let us all know the standards upon which we base our values.

Obviously, Mary could still make decisions without necessarily consulting Joseph. 'At that time, Mary arose and went with haste into the hill country to a town of Judah' (Amplified). What was she looking for? She was out to confirm the word of God. Sometimes we hear such things from God that we can only say that if it works out, then God must be in it. She went to see the physical confirmation. She was gripped maybe by fear, maybe by unbelief, maybe by nothing! She went in haste. Where was her inner peace? Some advocate strongly that when we hear from God, we have inner peace. Yes, it may eventually come (as in this case). Permit me to say that when sometimes it hits at first, against our initial knowledge of the word, peace flees. How many mistakes we can avoid when we take out time to confirm our visions and dreams with the Bible? Let me also say here that sometimes we might need to move into the 'hills' (a place where we can meet people to discuss and confirm the truth) to confirm certain things. Our prayers then may not be to hear again from God (though this is not wrong, once He speaks and twice we hear), but our prayers will be that God puts some physical things or people together to make things clearer to us. We can see that once Elisabeth prophesied to her and exhorted her to just believe, she went into song. When you are in the place where you discuss with people who had had encounters with God, people with sincere knowledge of God, to make a decision, you tend to forget your immediate challenge and worship God, for then your spirit man is aided to see things as God would see them.

Mary still had a problem; she could not just walk home. She stayed behind. Why? If it was to enjoy the presence of God and be in the atmosphere of the Spirit, it was not bad. If it was to wait for the right time it was not bad. If it was to see and confirm that these things were not dreams, it was not bad. She waited. She went to Elizabeth when she (Elizabeth) was already six months pregnant. She waited until she gave birth. She may have witnessed the miracle of restoration of the speech to Zacharias. Waiting is helpful. It gives us time to be ready emotionally. Then once we have fixed our minds, we can then move on. It gives us more confirmations. It gives us time to plan. Some people are so spiritual that they tend to forget that Jesus fell three times on the way to the cross. The ultimate job waited for him to struggle up and carry the cross again. Is it not obvious that it was when getting up for the third time was so painful that the soldiers had to find Simon of Cyrene to help him? These people do not even wait. Jesus could have flown to Golgotha with the cross. Time was necessary. It took all that time before this ultimate job for mankind could be done. No fast-forward.

John the Baptist was born. It had been three months since the encounter. Joseph must have been worried by then. He must have heard of the hastened departure. Was something wrong? Mary could no longer hide. She had to come out perhaps claiming scriptures. The gift of a man must make way for him. The righteous is as bold as a lion. It is well. Do you wonder how many promises she tried to claim? As she came down from the hills, she was reciting the entire Bible! What can we say? Did she go straight to Joseph? We cannot say. All we know is that there is nothing hidden that shall not be revealed. Joseph found out. The Bible reads, 'She was found . . .' So the rumour was true. The just man was confused. How many times have just men been confused before then and after then? Poor Joseph. He was truly just. He realized that the anger of man does not work the righteousness of God. He must be slow to anger. The servant of the Lord does not make haste.

> Therefore thus saith the Lord GOD, Behold, I lay in Zion for a foundation a stone, a tried stone, a precious corner stone, a sure foundation: he that believeth shall not make haste. (Isa. 28:16 KJV)

He must not act in revenge.

> Thou shalt not avenge, nor bear any grudge against the children of thy people, but thou shalt love thy neighbour as thyself: I am the LORD. (Lev. 19:18 KJV)

> Dearly beloved, avenge not yourselves, but rather give place unto wrath: for it is written, Vengeance is mine; I will repay, saith the Lord. (Rom. 12:19 KJV)

Some would say that the word of God must be fulfilled. She must die.

And having in a readiness to revenge all disobedience, when your obedience is fulfilled. (2 Cor. 10:6 KJV)

No, the same word of God also says we should show mercy. God is merciful.

Blessed are the merciful: for they shall obtain mercy. (Matt. 5:7 KJV)

Who will have all men to be saved, and to come unto the knowledge of the truth. (1 Tim. 2:4 KJV)

For thou, Lord, art good, and ready to forgive; and plenteous in mercy unto all them that call upon thee. (Ps. 86:5 KJV)

O give thanks to the Lord of lords: for his mercy endureth for ever. (Ps. 136:3 KJV)

And I prayed unto the LORD my God, and made my confession, and said, O Lord, the great and dreadful God, keeping the covenant and mercy to them that love him, and to them that keep his commandments. (Dan. 9:4 KJV)

There exists a need for us as believers to balance our understanding of the scriptures. When God has touched a man, when a man has been broken, when a man is totally gripped by Him, he sees mercy first. That man is gracious. He wishes to act, but in sensitivity to the Spirit, he is constrained by the love of Christ. He knows that it is the will of God that all should come to the knowledge of truth. Do you wonder why Jesus saved the woman caught in adultery? Do you wonder why he was quiet for a time and started to write on the ground? The entire being was put to test. We should all pray that the Lord should finish his work in us. We will begin to see our faults in others. This is the moulding of the Lord! It is the program of the Lord in us to make us shine as the light of the world. It is to purge us and make us vessels of honour. It kills the 'I' in us. Joseph saw the fault and felt the hurt, yet he would not want a public disgrace for Mary. This is the peak of Christianity and we should all pray to attain this height.

And, ye masters, do the same things unto them, forbearing threatening: knowing that your Master also is in heaven; neither is there respect of persons with him. (Eph. 6:9 KJV)

Forbearing one another, and forgiving one another, if any man have a quarrel against any: even as Christ forgave you, so also do ye. (Col. 3:13 KJV)

With all lowliness and meekness, with longsuffering, forbearing one another in love . . . (Eph. 4:2 KJV)

As for Mary, she was found guilty of a crime she did not commit, and she could not defend herself. Joseph probably saw her honesty but could not reconcile things. All Mary could do was to pray that the Lord should vindicate her. There was one option: Joseph should claim that he impregnated Mary. Joseph felt that he could not lie to protect her. Oh, how some Christians lie to protect others. No, it should not be. You cannot help God. Do you not remember the case of Uzzah, how he helped God? Yes, the ark became stable, yet God killed him. As spiritual as David was, he found it hard to understand. You cannot sin while 'helping' God. Joseph would not agree to lie to save her. No doubt he was hurt, but the just man would not lie or live in deceit. So he wanted to let Mary paddle her own canoe and do her cover-up by herself. The death of Mary did not make any sense to him, no doubt. At least he was going to sleep on it. Was he a weak man? No, not at all. He was not an indecisive man. He was a man touched by God. He was sensitive enough to know that there was something about what was going on so he did not need a hasty decision. He slept. Only few of us can sleep in such a situation. Let us envy him. If only we as Christians should direct our thoughts on things above, on Philippians 4:8, we would find out that we are able to wake up with solutions to our problems. Sleep is good. Some of us have such noisy and restless minds that we often go back to the office in our dreams. As for Joseph, he slept and woke up knowing what to do. The angel of the Lord had explained things to him in the dream.

The explanation was all he needed. If God says it, then it is so. It was an independent confirmation of what Mary had perhaps told him.

The book of Hebrews (Chapter 11) brings this out clearly: everyone acts by one's own faith. We need our own faith. Jesus said of the sower seed that some produce in thirty, some in sixty, and some a hundredfold. Whatever it is, we need our own faith. Leaders in church and parents should let faith of the children grow, teaching all to act in their individual faiths. In this way, none will look back like Lot's wife. Joseph combined this dream with the rest of the messages and with the scriptures, and he knew what to do. He, of course, thought of the salvation of Israel. This action was going to save people from sin. What is more scriptural? He woke up and obeyed. Let us not miss the point here. Not all dreams are from God. Some are from Satan, and some from us. There is only one acid test. It must not be against the known will of God—the Holy Scriptures.

He took her as his wife and did not make love with her, 'not till she had brought forth her firstborn son' (KJV). Some think this to mean that she still remained a virgin after she gave birth. Having said that, let us talk about the self-control of this man, which in fact sums up the man we are dealing with. How many people are eager to go off on a honeymoon just after the marriage ceremony? Isn't this almost unbelievable? This man was a man, indeed. Let me say here that it is not a function of the times they were in. The older generation tends to blame the vices of their time on the youths. Have they forgotten that from Cain, men have risen against brothers in cold murder? Or that from Abraham's time, homosexuality had been existing in Sodom and Gomorrah? Or that part of the laws of Moses was the death penalty on a man or woman who had sex with an animal? Am I excusing sin because it started long ago? No, God forbid! Do I support prostitution because there have been temple prostitutes from the beginning of time? Not at all! Let me quickly add that the older generation should not complain, because they are the ones making laws that remove God from our schools and our homes. I wish they knew that they are assisting the spirit of lawlessness in these last days by removing God and the Holy Scriptures from youth. Does it not surprise us all how we keep our children away from the Bible and prayer in schools, giving them condoms instead, and when they are in prisons, we give them Bibles? What do we think the Bible will do for them in prison? My answer would be nothing much.

Anyway, I am saying that Joseph was just being himself. It was Joseph, not the time. He was the one who decided he was not going to have sex with Mary. How many of us can do this? Do we think it was grace? Many have taken the grace of God in vain. How many times have we have wilfully disobeyed God? God have mercy on us all.

As for Mary, she did not cause a brother to stumble. She knew what was at stake. She surely wouldn't tempt him unnecessarily. Unlike Eve, she would not give a forbidden fruit to her husband. How many brethren have erred during courtship? Oh, that we may be more careful and plant the right seeds towards our marriages. Oh, that we please Him by keeping our bed undefiled.

After about nine months, she was to give to birth. The man was there. He was not watching a football match, not in the office, nor was he sleeping. This is the example of the very Son of God. I think it is worth emulating. This is how His only Son was born. Let us know that the hosts of heaven have been watching and monitoring things. They influenced Joseph to be right there at that time. If it were not important, it simply could have happened in any other way. Let us plan to be there when it happens. That was how the Son's birth took place. The hosts of heaven were monitoring this issue from start to finish. They made them to go to Bethlehem so the scriptures would be fulfilled. Do we think the Spirit and all heavenly hosts could not have made Mary give birth without the presence of Joseph? Let us as husbands make efforts to be available when it happens. If you can be right there, even better. Joseph had time for the wife. During her pains, a helping and dependable hand was there. This time he was not sleeping and dreaming. He knew when to sleep and when to be awake. Is there not a time for everything under the sun?

The last issue we want to talk about is that once they got married, God stopped dealing with Mary. All instructions were given to Joseph. Here again God was setting an example of how He expects us to run our homes. It did not matter whether Mary was a prophetess. It did not matter if she had even seen angels. It did not matter if she was highly favoured among all women. Where was all the 'Hail, thou that art highly favoured, the Lord is with thee: blessed art thou among women'? We cannot say she went to the background. We cannot say it was because

Joseph was a just man. We cannot say it was because Joseph was always obeying God. The God that said in the Garden of Eden, 'And thy desire shall be to thy husband, and he shall rule over thee' was at work. He would not speak to Mary to tell her husband. Before she was married, angels went to her directly. She consented directly to God. Now she was to consent indirectly. I feel this is an example to note. Again, we cannot relegate the example of this monitored family to the background. God started giving instructions to Joseph and expected Mary to obey. This is what Paul tried to say when in Ephesians he talked about wives submitting to their husbands:

> *Submitting yourselves one to another in the fear of God.*
> *Wives, submit yourselves unto your own husbands, as unto the Lord.*
> *For the husband is the head of the wife, even as Christ is the head of the church: and he is the saviour of the body.*
> *Therefore as the church is subject unto Christ, so let the wives be to their own husbands in every thing.*
> *Husbands, love your wives, even as Christ also loved the church, and gave himself for it; that he might sanctify and cleanse it with the washing of water by the word,*
> *that he might present it to himself a glorious church, not having spot, or wrinkle, or any such thing; but that it should be holy and without blemish.*
> *So ought men to love their wives as their own bodies. He that loveth his wife loveth himself.*
> *For no man ever yet hated his own flesh; but nourisheth and cherisheth it, even as the Lord the church:*
> *For we are members of his body, of his flesh, and of his bones.*
> *For this cause shall a man leave his father and mother, and shall be joined unto his wife, and they two shall be one flesh.*
> *This is a great mystery: but I speak concerning Christ and the church.*
> *Nevertheless let every one of you in particular so love his wife even as himself; and the wife see that she reverence her husband.* (Eph. 5:21-33 KJV)
> *Wives, submit yourselves unto your own husbands, as it is fit in the Lord.* (Col. 3:18 KJV)

While saying this, we should be careful not to miss the point. Jesus sent Mary Magdalene to be the first evangelist. We are not saying here that woman cannot be called of God. What we are saying is that God respects the man as the head of the home. In Deuteronomy, a husband or father, respectively, can annul a vow by the wife or a daughter.

And Moses spake unto the heads of the tribes concerning the children of Israel, saying, This is the thing which the LORD hath commanded. (Num. 30:1 KJV)

If a woman also vow a vow unto the LORD, and bind herself by a bond, being in her father's house in her youth; (Num. 30:3 KJV)

But if her father disallow her in the day that he heareth; not any of her vows, or of her bonds wherewith she hath bound her soul, shall stand: and the LORD shall forgive her, because her father disallowed her.

And if she had at all an husband, when she vowed, or uttered ought out of her lips, wherewith she bound her soul; (Num. 30:5-6 KJV)

But if her husband hath utterly made them void on the day he heard them; then whatsoever proceeded out of her lips concerning her vows, or concerning the bond of her soul, shall not stand: her husband hath made them void; and the LORD shall forgive her. (Num. 30:12 KJV)

Every vow, and every binding oath to afflict the soul, her husband may establish it, or her husband may make it void. (Num. 30:13 KJV)

What do we say to that? God is interested in our homes and family authority. Nowadays what do we see? We see governments enacting laws against the homes and children. We see contract marriages. We see divorces. We see insubordination. How do we explain all these in the light of this story?

1.3 *Mending the fence*

Let us conclude this section of the book with the story below.

> *And when he came to his disciples, he saw a great multitude about them, and the scribes questioning with them. And straightway all the people, when they beheld him, were greatly amazed, and running to him saluted him. And he asked the scribes, What question ye with them? And one of the multitude answered and said, Master, I have brought unto thee my son, which hath a dumb spirit; And wheresoever he taketh him, he teareth him: and he foameth, and gnasheth with his teeth, and pineth away: and I spake to thy disciples that they should cast him out; and they could not. He answereth him, and saith, O faithless generation, how long shall I be with you? how long shall I suffer you? bring him unto me. And they brought him unto him: and when he saw him, straightway the spirit tare him; and he fell on the ground, and wallowed foaming. And he asked his father, How long is it ago since this came unto him? And he said, Of a child. And ofttimes it hath cast him into the fire, and into the waters, to destroy him: but if thou canst do any thing, have compassion on us, and help us. Jesus said unto him, If thou canst believe, all things are possible to him that believeth. And straightway the father of the child cried out, and said with tears, Lord, I believe; help thou mine unbelief. When Jesus saw that the people came running together, he rebuked the foul spirit, saying unto him, Thou dumb and deaf spirit, I charge thee, come out of him, and enter no more into him. And the spirit cried, and rent him sore, and came out of him: and he was as one dead; insomuch that many said, He is dead.* (Mark 9:14-26 KJV)

The Bible explains that the thief comes to steal and kill and destroy. It does not matter how much has been stolen and taken from you. The enemy meant it to have been worse as with the story above. The good news is that just in like the story above, though you have been thrown into water and fire since you were born, God has preserved you. You may not have been able to climb up to the mountains to meet Jesus; He has come down to see you. Today is the day of salvation. Rise up and seek the Master. Tell him you believe. He will help your unbelief.

He will stretch His hand; He will save you from the mess. Even if people have said your marriage is dead, Jesus will stretch out His hand and it will live again.

Are you yet to know Him? Why do you not want to accept Him? He loves you more than you can imagine. Why do you think you are in control? No man wins by strength alone. Invite him to be your Lord and master. He will empower you to be His child.

2

Questions about money
in the church

2.1   Introduction

> *For the time will come when they will not endure sound doctrine; but*
> *after their own lusts shall they heap to themselves teachers, having*
> *itching ears; And they shall turn away their ears from the truth, and*
> *shall be turned unto fables.* (2 Tim. 4:3-4 KJV)

This instruction to Timothy by Paul is more aflame today than it was
then. For this time we are in, Jesus gave some everlasting advice:

> *And ye shall know the truth, and the truth shall make you free.*
> (John 8:32 KJV)

It is evident that it is only when we know the truth that we can
contend for our faith. We all need to know what we believe in.
These days, we find a lot of Christians who do not read the Bible.
Some believe every word their ministers tell them because we have
been told that they must not query anointing. If the only thing this
section of this book does to the reader is make him resolve to study
the Bible thoroughly, then it has succeeded. The style of the section,
therefore, is questioning. This will make us reach our own conclusion
by ourselves.

This section delves into a hot area in the church. Money! We will look
at Bible verses and ask questions. Sometimes answers are provided;
sometimes they are not. Sometimes these answers may be wrong.

Other times, the answers are not known. It is my desire that as we read through, we make up our minds on sound doctrine.

First we will look at tithes and then at how Jesus had money to run His ministry as well as the early church. Finally, we will look at vows.

2.2　*Speaking out the truth*

Almost everyone I discussed these topics with had, by default, the initial response 'Do not speak against anointed men of God.' They just do not understand how I can say that men of God are not using money well in the church. It must be sedition. There is this sad notion in the church today that anything said from the altar is infallible. Indeed, this is supposed to be so. Unfortunately, the ones who stand at the altars do not want to correct this notion, because they gain from the belief.

So the first issue we would like to look at is that of speaking against the anointed men of God. We are not here disrespecting them. The question is, is it right to say that what a man of God is doing is not correct? If we see an anointed pastor stealing, can we say he is stealing without dishonouring anointing? Is it wrong for us to attempt to seek answers to these sorts of questions? The Bible says of Andrew the apostle,

> *Again the next day after John stood, and two of his disciples; And looking upon Jesus as he walked, he saith, Behold the Lamb of God! And the two disciples heard him speak, and they followed Jesus. Then Jesus turned, and saw them following, and saith unto them, What seek ye? They said unto him, Rabbi, (which is to say, being interpreted, Master,) where dwellest thou? He saith unto them, Come and see. They came and saw where he dwelt, and abode with him that day: for it was about the tenth hour. One of the two which heard John speak, and followed him, was Andrew, Simon Peter's brother. (John 1:35–39 KJV)*

He was first John's disciple. Then John showed him the way, and he left John the Baptist to follow Jesus. This mind evaluates the truth and follows the truth. While we may be careful about what we hear, we must always renew our minds on the truth that we believe. The Matthew version of the parable of the sower makes this clear. If we do not understand what we believe, then it is just a matter of time before the devil confuses us.

> *So listen to the meaning of that story about the farmer. What is the seed that fell by the road? That seed is like the person who hears the teaching about the kingdom but does not understand it. The Evil One comes and takes away the things that were planted in that person's heart. And what is the seed that fell on rocky ground? That seed is like the person who hears the teaching and quickly accepts it with joy. But he does not let the teaching go deep into his life. He keeps it only a short time. When trouble or persecution comes because of the teaching he accepted, then he quickly gives up. And what is the seed that fell among the thorny weeds? That seed is like the person who hears the teaching but lets worries about this life and love of money stop that teaching from growing. So the teaching does not produce fruit in that person's life. But what is the seed that fell on the good ground? That seed is like the person who hears the teaching and understands it. That person grows and produces fruit, sometimes 100 times more, sometimes 60 times more, and sometimes 30 times more.* (Matt. 13:18–23 ICB)

Why are we being discouraged from understating the truth? If we cannot ask questions, we cannot understand the truth. There is this joke from children's Sunday school:

> The teacher says, 'We must confess our sins to be forgiven.'
> A child asks, 'What of dumb people who cannot talk?'

Why should we not ask questions to understand? Jesus said we need to understand to produce fruit. How do we understand without asking questions? God told us we must teach the word to our children. How do we teach without asking questions? How can we understand if we are to accept everything from the altar as being right? As you read along, you may want to ask if I am disrespecting anointed men of God. I like to say *no!* I am only compelled to talk about what is right and what is wrong. We shall look at three passages from the Bible and then attempt to draw some conclusions.

The first passage is in Exodus, where Moses told God that He (God) was not right!

> *And the Lord said to Moses, "Go down from this mountain. Your people, the people you brought out of the land of Egypt, have done a terrible sin. They have quickly turned away from the things I commanded them to do. They have made for themselves a calf of melted gold. They have worshiped that calf and offered sacrifices to it. The people have said, 'Israel, these are your gods who brought you out of Egypt.'" The Lord said to Moses, "I have seen these people. I know that they are very stubborn people. So now do not stop me. I am so angry with them that I am going to destroy them. Then I will make you and your descendants a great nation." But Moses begged the Lord his God. Moses said, "Lord, don't let your anger destroy your people. You brought these people out of Egypt with your great power and strength. Don't let the people of Egypt say, 'The Lord brought the Israelites out of Egypt. But he planned to kill them in the mountains and destroy them from the earth.' So stop being angry. Don't destroy your people. Remember the men who served you—Abraham, Isaac and Israel. You promised with an oath to them. You said, 'I will make your descendants as many as the stars in the sky. I will give your descendants all this land that I have promised them. It will be theirs forever.'" So the Lord changed his mind. He did not destroy the people as he had said he might. Then Moses went down the mountain. In his hands he had the two stone tablets with the agreement on them. The commands were written on both sides of each stone, front and back. God himself had made the stones. And God himself had written the commands on the stones.*
> (Exod. 32:7-16 ICB)

> *The next day Moses told the people, "You have done a terrible sin. But now I will go up to the Lord. Maybe I can do something so your sins will be removed. Then you will belong to God again."*

So Moses went back to the Lord and said, "How terrible it is! These people have sinned horribly. They have made for themselves gods from gold. Now, forgive them of this sin. If you will not, then erase my name. Erase it from the book in which you have written the names of your people." But the Lord told Moses, "I will erase from my book the names of the people who sin against me. So now, go. Lead the people where I have told you. My angel will lead you. When the time comes to punish, I will punish them for their sin." So the Lord caused terrible things to happen to the people. He did this because of what they did with the calf Aaron had made. (Exod. 32: 30-35 ICB)

Moses made some points in this passage: (1) That the people are God's people not Moses'; (2) Unbelievers will misunderstand this action of yours; (3) You are very angry; (4) Remember your promises. He was standing before God and speaking to God as if speaking to a man. He may have spoken even wrong things, but when we deal with God (the source of anointing), he looks at the heart. He was not just talking so everyone would know he succeeded as a leader. That would have been selfish. Indeed, he had keyed into the very war of the universe. For God to win, he was ready to lay down his life and go to hell. Here we have a man telling God that what He was about to do was not correct.

What do we have today? What do we hear today? What do men say today? Do not speak against the anointed as if anointing and evil can agree. The test is, is what we are saying true? Are we saying the truth because of a selfish hidden agenda? To say that we must not talk at all because of anointing is defeating the essence of the anointing: holiness. Anointing and sin can never mix.

The second example is about Jesus and the high priest:

The high priest asked Jesus questions about his followers and his teaching. Jesus answered, "I have spoken openly to everyone. I have always taught in synagogues and in the Temple, where all the Jews come together. I never said anything in secret. So why do you question me? Ask the people who heard my teaching. They know what I said." When Jesus said this, one of the guards standing there hit him. The guard said, "Is that the way you answer the high priest?" Jesus answered him, "If I said something wrong, then say what was wrong. But if what I said is true, why do you hit me?" (John 18:19-23 ICB)

The answer Jesus gave to the high priest was perceived as wrong. The same accusation we have today: why do you speak to the anointed of God like that? The problem is that we always want to exalt an office beyond good and bad. This should never be done. Let us look at the answer of the real high priest.

'Have I said something wrong?' This is the litmus test, when we say something that looks like insult to the anointed man. Then is there a wrong hidden agenda? What we say goes beyond what is said. Jesus says that from the heart come all issues of life. God deals with the heart. By Him, all actions are weighed. Therefore, the right frame of mind that can stand before God must be the mind from which every statement is made. Are we saying something that is plain, simple, and bad? Otherwise, if we have a hidden cause and we are just using good and bad as a cover-up, then we are undeniably immoral and must not speak against the anointed. Truth, they say, is bitter, so care must be taken to administer it. Otherwise, you can be accused, distracting from the truth. Evidently, if it takes another man to tell you what is bad, as an anointed man, then you have already rebelled against the Holy Spirit. Little wonder, therefore, that woe betides the man that confronts with the truth, the anointed man who, in the first case, is hurting inside. It is probably a self-image preservation syndrome. No matter how we say it, our judgement is already passed: *Crucify him.* Jesus did not say something wrong, and he did not say it wrongly, yet he was crucified. So we may as well say the truth anyhow, as long as our intents and consciences are clear. Notwithstanding, we must avoid confrontation. For the man of God must not strive. The Bible says that we must live at peace with all men as long as it depends on us (Heb. 12:14). If you are superior or equals, just say it. If you are junior, you may want to count the cost. Or better still, get someone trusted who is superior to say it. We must speak the truth one to another, at any rate.

Despite the consequences, we must say the truth. The son of man must sound the trumpet. John the Baptist spoke out and lost his head. The truth remained. Truth can never be killed. It may be suppressed, but with time, it will always come out. Standing by the truth comes with its own hazards. All the same, it must be said. Truth is truth, bitter or sweet. We must strive to say it as nicely as we can. If we must say it, say it we must.

The third passage is that of Paul's confrontation with the high priest.

> *Paul looked at the Jewish council and said, "Brothers, I have lived my life in a good way before God up to this day." Ananias, the high priest, heard this and told the men who were standing near Paul to hit him on his mouth. Paul said to Ananias, "God will hit you too! You are like a wall that has been painted white! You sit there and judge me, using the law of Moses. But you are telling them to hit me, and that is against the law."*
> *The men standing near Paul said to him, "You cannot talk like that to God's high priest! You are insulting him!"*
> *Paul said, "Brothers, I did not know this man was the high priest. It is written in the Scriptures, 'You must not curse a leader of your people.'"* (Acts 23:1-5 ICB)

Paul said to a high priest that God would hit him too; he was cursing a high priest! Was there sin in what was said? Did he say a wrong thing? Was it out of anger and revenge? Was this wrong to say to anybody, for that matter? It is clear that what was said, in general, was not right. And it was said wrongly. Do we see why Paul apologised for this?

In conclusion, we see Moses telling God that He was 'wrong'. With the right motive and right words, the source of anointing did not count this as sin. As it came down to Jesus and the high priest, Jesus was accused even when he was right. Today we argue, 'Do not even talk. Just keep quiet.' If you have the right motive before God, say the truth but try to say it in a nice way, knowing that even the nicest way can be punished by the 'anointed man of God'.

It is actually on this foundation that I set out to write this book—to ask questions about what is right with the noblest spirit and mind. I also wanted to stir the right mind of questioning and produce noble Christians, like the Berean ones, who can tell the preachers to wait until they have read the scriptures by themselves. I have even quoted many Bible versions in this book so there will be no need to keep opening the Bible whilst reading the book. Of course, if you decide to read it in your own Bible, then my goal of getting people to study and cross-reference by themselves is achieved.

When a preacher talks about money in the church, you make a quick reference to the right passages in the Bible and demand that proper explanations be made. I hope also that preachers, when they come up to talk about money (and indeed all the 'ministers' that feel they must preach before an offering is made in the church), will always put at the backs of their minds that someone has written a book on this and will then attempt to preach the truth. Until we ask the right questions, we can never understand. Until we understand, we cannot produce the right fruit. Look at how many questions Jesus asked his disciples at a time.

And when Jesus knew it, he saith unto them, Why reason ye, because ye have no bread? perceive ye not yet, neither understand? have ye your heart yet hardened? Having eyes, see ye not? and having ears, hear ye not? and do ye not remember? When I brake the five loaves among five thousand, how many baskets full of fragments took ye up? They say unto him, Twelve. And when the seven among four thousand, how many baskets full of fragments took ye up? And they said, Seven. And he said unto them, How is it that ye do not understand? (Mark 8:17-21 KJV)

2.3   Tithe

We start by looking at the very beginning. The style is to look at each verse about tithes and then explain the passage as it is. The aim is to take one fact after another. Precept upon precept! We shall do this by answering one question at a time from our sets of questions:

- What is a tithe?
- Who pays a tithe?
- To whom is a tithe paid?
- When do we pay a tithe?
- What is the content of a tithe?
- What is the role of the one who receives a tithe?

Let us start from the book of Genesis:

> And Melchizedek king of Salem brought forth bread and wine: and he was the priest of the most high God. And he blessed him, and said, Blessed be Abram of the most high God, possessor of heaven and earth: And blessed be the most high God, which hath delivered thine enemies into thy hand. And he gave him tithes of all. And the king of Sodom said unto Abram, Give me the persons, and take the goods to thyself. (Gen. 14:18-21 KJV)

What is a tithe? This is very simple. Rather, let us keep it simple for now, for as we move on, this seemingly simple question becomes so complex and unanswerable. Tithe is a tenth: if you divide it into ten equal portions, tithe is one portion.

Who pays a tithe? The man who has got income from which to pay tithes. In this case, Abraham. It is important to observe that the servants did not pay. I have heard some preachers encouraging payment of tithe of what you hope or are praying to have as a demonstration of faith. This is not represented in this example.

To whom is a tithe paid? He paid tithe to a priest of God. They say in our days that a priest of God is a minister. Can it not also be the normal Christian? For indeed, are we not a peculiar people and royal priesthood? We are priest now, and we will be called priest later.

> Ye also, as lively stones, are built up a spiritual house, an holy priesthood, to offer up spiritual sacrifices, acceptable to God by Jesus Christ. But ye are a chosen generation, a royal priesthood, an holy nation, a peculiar people; that ye should show forth the praises of him who hath called you out of darkness into his marvellous light: (1 Peter 2:5, 9 KJV)

And hath made us kings and priests unto God and his Father; to him be glory and dominion for ever and ever. Amen. (Rev. 1:6 KJV)

And hast made us unto our God kings and priests: and we shall reign on the earth. (Rev. 5:10 KJV)

Blessed and holy is he that hath part in the first resurrection: on such the second death hath no power, but they shall be priests of God and of Christ, and shall reign with him a thousand years. (Rev. 20:6 KJV)

If we say this priest was a special priest, are we not going to make things complicated? Who is and how do we know a special priest today?

When do you pay tithe? We don't have enough information in this passage to declare that he was always paying tithe or that this was the only time he paid tithe. If he did, to whom did he always pay the tithes? Can we build this doctrine on this one case? Apostle Paul, when he referred to this event in Hebrews, did not portray a continuous event. For this one example, he paid tithe of his increase. He paid of only the goods he had recovered. To Abraham, he was dissociated from wealth. He needed to shine as light to the world around him. He needed to live a blameless life. He needed to be an example of the believer in conduct. He was not prepared for his good to be evil spoken of or bring God to reproach. Do you recall that among these people were Lot and his servants, who strove with Abraham's servants? Do you recall that Abraham was left to fate while Lot took over the greener and well-watered pastures? This is no wealth of the infidel handed to us. When integrity in God was on one side and attachment to wealth stood on the other side, he chose God. How eager it is for ministers and the church of today to talk about tithe in this passage without regards to this truth written for our admonition and perfection. Please recall that Joshua and his men destroyed this city when they came to occupy the land after many years. The king of Jerusalem was among the five kings killed (Josh. 12:10). Again, it is not as if Abraham took

90 per cent for himself and gave 10 per cent to God. He did not take anything. A lot of us are not aware of this fact.

What is the content of tithe? We cannot say what the content was except for assumptions. We may say it was livestock and maybe money (gold, silver, and so forth). This is only an assumption. We cannot build our case that tithe contains money on assumption, nor can we say that tithing does not involve money.

What is the role of the one who receives tithe? The priest brought them bread and wine. Clearly, everyone has a role. These men coming from war were entertained. Do you know the number of men that went to war and how much bread and wine was required? The priest gave too before he received the tithe. The priest already had resources from which to give. Whether it was his personal money or money from the storehouse—he used to entertain men coming from war—is another matter. It is safer to assume that it was his personal money. Otherwise, we will make things complex too early if we think that men of war (workers, or maybe unbelievers) ate tithe! He prayed, then he gave, not just spiritual feeding but also physical feeding. This is different from what we have today.

Today most ministers want full-time eating from the house of God. No work. No skill. Nothing. They are only given. They do not give. All they want is to be given. Another thing we must learn is that the priest cared? How much do we care today as ministers? Why do you have the best car, house, food, and clothes, yet in your own church, not to mention the whole world, there are people dying of hunger and disease. Do we not think ministers should wake up? Are we not ashamed that the church is not in the forefront of caring in this world, knowing that the last day Jesus is going to separate the sheep from the goat based on how much each cared for humanity? What do we find? Ministers just sit back, eat, and quarrel over who is eating more. The truth is, when you see quarrels like these, check out the minister. Sometimes he had nothing before he became a minister. He had no skill, no education, and no work before he came to the service of God. I honestly wonder if any of the apostles did not have some form of employment before they came into full-time ministry. Of course, I cannot say that anyone should not serve God.

This is the next passage I would like us to study:

> *And all the tithe of the land, whether of the seed of the land, or of the fruit of the tree, is the LORD'S: it is holy unto the LORD. And if a man will at all redeem ought of his tithes, he shall add thereto the fifth part thereof. And concerning the tithe of the herd, or of the flock, even of whatsoever passeth under the rod, the tenth shall be holy unto the LORD. He shall not search whether it be good or bad, neither shall he change it: and if he change it at all, then both it and the change thereof shall be holy; it shall not be redeemed. These are the commandments, which the LORD commanded Moses for the children of Israel in mount Sinai. (Lev. 27:30-34 KJV)*

What is tithe? Again, let us stick to this one-tenth definition.

Who pays tithe? These commands are clearly said here to be for the people of Israel. This is where we have to be careful. I do not intend to be a theologian or professor explaining what should be for the modern Christian of today. The rule is simple: if we want to go back to the Old Testament, as children of Israel, let us go back to all. My observation is usually that when we go back to the Old Testament, we go back to the portion with money and giving. We take tithe but not other laws like wave offering and meat offerings. We take tithe and we leave robes, incense, and altars. Why? This command here is for the people of Israel. Some people say we are the spiritual Israel of today. Is money spiritual?

To whom is tithe paid? This was for the Lord. Is this not simple enough—or do I say complex enough? Where is God today? He is that hungry man, that sick man, that man in the prison, that naked man, that homeless man. He may also be the minister on a personal jet. Look at this verse from Jesus himself:

> *Then the King will say to the good people on his right, 'Come. My Father has given you his blessing. Come and receive the kingdom*

God has prepared for you since the world was made. I was hungry,
and you gave me food. I was thirsty, and you gave me something to
drink. I was alone and away from home, and you invited me into
your house. I was without clothes, and you gave me something to
wear. I was sick, and you cared for me. I was in prison, and you
visited me.' Then the good people will answer, 'Lord, when did we
see you hungry and give you food? When did we see you thirsty and
give you something to drink? When did we see you alone and away
from home and invite you into our house? When did we see you
without clothes and give you something to wear? When did we see
you sick or in prison and care for you?' Then the King will answer,
'I tell you the truth. Anything you did for any of my people here,
you also did for me.' (Matt. 25:34-40 ICB)

In the Old Testament, it was Levites. In the New Testament it is any
born-again person. In fact, not just born again, but all men according
to Paul. Jesus said;

Whoever helps one of these little ones because they are my followers
will truly get his reward. He will get his reward even if he only gave
my follower a cup of cold water. (Matt 10:42 ICB)

When do you pay tithe? From the passage above, it is obvious that it
was seasonal.

What is the content of a tithe? We see it clearly: crops and animals. Was
everyone in Israel into agriculture at this time? *No!* From Genesis, we
know that some had become fighters, industrialists, moneylenders,
and so forth. Some even helped in building the tent and making the
Levites' robes. God gave these people special talents. These people
were not paying tents as their one-tenth! Tithes were crops and
animals. Doing well to men is beyond crops and animals, as we see
above from Jesus' statements. Men who Paul describes as hungry for
filthy lucre have zoomed into tithing in our modern church. They are
in the gospel business for money and personal gains. Jude said it is the
madness of prophets. Do you see how God discouraged turning His
temple into a den of thieves by enacting that 120 per cent be paid if

you want to bring in money and not the crops? His temple today is not a place of prayer.

Other facts? This place addresses the right heart when giving. Give not to your benefit. Do not give the bad ones and keep the good ones. Serve God in sincerity and truth. Give in sincerity and truth.

Let us move on to the next passage:

> *And the LORD spake unto Aaron, Thou shalt have no inheritance in their land, neither shalt thou have any part among them: I am thy part and thine inheritance among the children of Israel. And, behold, I have given the children of Levi all the tenth in Israel for an inheritance, for their service which they serve, even the service of the tabernacle of the congregation. Neither must the children of Israel henceforth come nigh the tabernacle of the congregation, lest they bear sin, and die. But the Levites shall do the service of the tabernacle of the congregation, and they shall bear their iniquity: it shall be a statute for ever throughout your generations, that among the children of Israel they have no inheritance. But the tithes of the children of Israel, which they offer as an heave offering unto the LORD, I have given to the Levites to inherit: therefore I have said unto them, Among the children of Israel they shall have no inheritance. And the LORD spake unto Moses, saying, Thus speak unto the Levites, and say unto them, When ye take of the children of Israel the tithes which I have given you from them for your inheritance, then ye shall offer up an heave offering of it for the LORD, even a tenth part of the tithe. And this your heave offering shall be reckoned unto you, as though it were the corn of the threshingfloor, and as the fulness of the winepress. Thus ye also shall offer an heave offering unto the LORD of all your tithes, which ye receive of the children of Israel; and ye shall give thereof the LORD'S heave offering to Aaron the priest. Out of all your gifts ye shall offer every heave offering of the LORD, of all the best thereof, even the hallowed part thereof out of it. Therefore thou shalt say unto them, When ye have heaved the best thereof from it, then it shall be counted unto the Levites as the increase of the threshingfloor, and as the increase of the winepress. And ye shall eat it in every place, ye and your households: for it is*

your reward for your service in the tabernacle of the congregation.
And ye shall bear no sin by reason of it, when ye have heaved from
it the best of it: neither shall ye pollute the holy things of the children
of Israel, lest ye die. (Num. 18:20-32 KJV)

What is a tithe? It is again clear here that it is a tenth.

Who pays a tithe? A tithe is given by the children of Israel.

To whom is tithe paid? God said it should be given to the Levites.
The Levites give your tithe to the priest. Why did God say this?
To compensate the Levites for their service in the tabernacle. God
effectively was saying, "Because these people work for me, I want
them to concentrate on their work; I want them to be compensated."
Do you notice they are not to get any other thing outside the tithe?
This is their only portion. No seed of faith! No laying some at the
apostle's feet. Do you also notice they are not to own anything: car,
house, and so on?

Today they say that our Levites are our modern workers in the church
(not just the ministers and their wives). Anyone who works full time
in the church must have access to the tithe. They must be paid. This is
the compensation for their work. What is the minister's work? Preach,
encourage, counsel, visit, teach, and so on. How does he do this?
Through messages from the altar, books, tapes recorded, songs, and
so forth. My question is why does the minister double-dip? He eats
the tithe and sells his books, tapes, and prayers (indeed some ministers
demand money before they pray for you or sell olive oil that they have
prayed over). What right has he to make merchandise of the word of
God? He is double-dipping and needs to repent. What right has the
gospel artist to sell his album and then still be paid by the church?
Now even if we are not paid for full-time work in the church, I ask
one disturbing question: what is our motive for writing that book or
preaching that message on tape? Is it that we want to make money?
Or is it that we want people to be saved and nurtured in the way of
God? It has to be one or the other because we cannot serve God
and mammon. If it is that we want people to be saved, then why can
we not do it for free, or even worse, for the cost price? If this is our

contribution for the souls of men, are we saying that we cannot do that for God and know that we have played our role in his kingdom? *Did I hear the mouth of the ox that threshed should not be muzzled?* (Deut. 25:4) Let the ox decide not to eat even when its mouth is open. How will the ministers eat? Let them work. Have they done as much as apostle Paul did, who took up a secular work in his days. He worked with Priscilla and Aquillia, some other Christians. With all that, he still has more to his credit than we do. Do we not see why our songs can no longer win battle and our harps, like David's, can no longer cast out demons? We sing for money. The money to invite these ministers to come to preach or sing is more than what some CEOs of companies earn. Yet they say they are ministering. No! They are working for money. Let the church wake up! If you work full time in your church, get paid by the church and let your albums be free. If you want to work outside the church singing and preaching, you have your conscience to deal with, for you must explain what you do for money and what you do for God. You cannot serve God and money. Jesus said it is impossible. This same Jesus is going to be the judge on the last day. I do not think he will change his words then.

What is the content of tithe? It is clear again what it is. Crops! Please recall that from the time of Nimrod, people have been involved in all forms of occupations. Even Moses was said to be taught, by teachers, the science of Egypt. Our apostle Paul was a tent builder. We know that despite other occupations, only the crops and animals were tithed. I am not surprised that in the Lord's Prayer, Jesus mentioned only food. No clothes. No money. Just food!

What do you do with tithe? It was meant for their welfare—welfare of those who work full time for God. This is where the righteous soul is vexed. What does the church use tithe money for today? It builds universities that are not free, not even for the full-time ministers. Their fees are higher than the secular ones sometimes. If schools, hospitals, and houses are set up using tithe money, then they must be free for all, or at least for full-time workers. I am sure that if normal life responsibilities were taken care of by tithing, most ministers would be sincere in their requests for money. By the way, why do men say they are called of God to be ministers, yet they are not ready to count the cost or make sacrifice? What do we think Paul meant when he said that for the sake of the gospel, you might remain unmarried. What do we think Jesus meant when he said that some made themselves eunuchs for the gospel sake? There is a price. We see a lot of people jump into the full ministry, and down the line, life is hard; they result to all sort of tricks to get money out of people. This is where I get so confused—why should a minister be thinking of what to eat and how to provide for his family? In the first case, the Bible says a minister who is married should fend for his household. In essence, he should have his source of money before becoming a minister. If you are a gospel singer, are you singing to minister to people or as a professional? The kingdom of God is not meat and drink. If we want to be rewarded in heaven, then why are we reaping our reward here on Earth? We work for God by ministering in songs and get paid by the church. If we think the money is not enough, we should find something else to do. In fact, a person is not supposed to be a minister unless he can fend for his family. He should come out and tell us what he is doing for money and what he is doing for God. Why will a minister pray to God, 'Take over my lips as minister to your people . . .' and then sell that tape? They are selling the word of God. Whatever we do (whether singers, pastors, maintenance crews, audio, and what have you), what are we doing for money, and what are we doing for God? We need to be able to separate what we say we do for God from what we do for money to live.

Let us move on to another passage:

> Then there shall be a place which the LORD your God shall choose to cause his name to dwell there; thither shall ye bring all that I command you; your burnt offerings, and your sacrifices, your tithes, and the heave offering of your hand, and all of your choice vows which ye vow unto the LORD: And ye shall rejoice before the LORD your God, ye, and your sons, and your daughters, and your menservants, and your maidservants, and the Levite that is within your gates; forasmuch as he hath no part nor inheritance with you. Take heed to thyself that thou offer not thy burnt offerings in every place that thou seest: But in the place which the LORD shall choose in one of thy tribes, there thou shalt offer thy burnt offerings, and

there thou shalt do all that I command thee. Notwithstanding thou mayest kill and eat flesh in all thy gates, whatsoever thy soul lusteth after, according to the blessing of the LORD thy God which he hath given thee: the unclean and the clean may eat thereof, as of the roebuck, and as of the hart. Only ye shall not eat the blood; ye shall pour it upon the earth as water. Thou mayest not eat within thy gates the tithe of thy corn, or of thy wine, or of thy oil, or the firstlings of thy herds or of thy flock, nor any of thy vows which thou vowest, nor thy freewill offerings, or heave offering of thine hand: But thou must eat them before the LORD thy God in the place which the LORD thy God shall choose, thou, and thy son, and thy daughter, and thy manservant, and thy maidservant, and the Levite that is within thy gates: and thou shalt rejoice before the LORD thy God in all that thou puttest thine hands unto. Take heed to thyself that thou forsake not the Levite as long as thou livest upon the earth. When the LORD thy God shall enlarge thy border, as he hath promised thee, and thou shalt say, I will eat flesh, because thy soul longeth to eat flesh; thou mayest eat flesh, whatsoever thy soul lusteth after. (Deut. 12:11-20 KJV)

Thou shalt truly tithe all the increase of thy seed, that the field bringeth forth year by year. And thou shalt eat before the LORD thy God, in the place which he shall choose to place his name there, the tithe of thy corn, of thy wine, and of thine oil, and the firstlings of thy herds and of thy flocks; that thou mayest learn to fear the LORD thy God always. (Deut. 14:22-23 KJV)

What is tithe? Life has become complicated. This tithe is to be eaten! What is this tithe that is eaten? Some say, it is a second tithe. For a second tithe, it is as follows:

First tithe: 100 x 1/10 = 10,
so you now have 90 remaining.
Second tithe: 90 x 1/10 = 9,
so you now have 81 remaining.

This means you have given 19 per cent as tithe. You are spending another 9 per cent as tithe just on religious buzz. Thank God we are not under the law. Some say it is the same tithe. This would mean that we need to distinguish which one we eat and which one we give to the Levites. Is there enough information for us to take this call? Must I engage in religious buzz with it? Can I not just keep the money and thank Jesus?

Other facts? I'd like to say here that mention is made of burnt offerings, which the present church will not talk about. I still wonder why we pick up only tithe and leave burnt offerings. Paul said that if we want the law, we must go back to all of it. Why are we not doing just that?

> *For as many as are of the works of the law are under the curse: for it is written, Cursed is every one that continueth not in all things which are written in the book of the law to do them.* (Gal. 3:10 KJV)

The next passage:

> *At the end of three years thou shalt bring forth all the tithe of thine increase the same year, and shalt lay it up within thy gates: And the Levite, (because he hath no part nor inheritance with thee,) and the stranger, and the fatherless, and the widow, which are within thy gates, shall come, and shall eat and be satisfied; that the LORD thy God may bless thee in all the work of thine hand which thou doest.* (Deut. 14:28-29 KJV)

> *When thou hast made an end of tithing all the tithes of thine increase the third year, which is the year of tithing, and hast given it unto the Levite, the stranger, the fatherless, and the widow, that they may eat within thy gates, and be filled; Then thou shalt say before the LORD thy God, I have brought away the hallowed things out of mine house, and also have given them unto the Levite, and unto the stranger, to the fatherless, and to the widow, according to all thy commandments which thou hast commanded me: I have not transgressed thy commandments, neither have I forgotten them.* (Deut. 26:12-13 KJV)

What is tithe? Some argue that this is a third type of tithe. Others say it is how tithing was practised every third year. Confusion! Either way, it marvels me that the church is not practising the whole tithing tradition, not to mention the whole law. I do not care if it is a third tithe or not. Suppose it is as follows:

First tithe: 100 x 1/10 = 10,
so you now have 90 remaining.
Second tithe: 90 x1/10 = 9,
so you now have 81 remaining.
Third tithe: 81 x 1/10 = 8.1,
So you now have 72.9 remaining

This implies that somewhere along the line, you should have given 27.1 per cent as tithe or maybe a straight 30 per cent as tithe (for those people who preach, why do mathematics with God!). Why is it that the church does not preach giving of tithes to widows and strangers? Again, if it is the same tithe, we must distinguish what part of the tithe we give to Levites (first tithing), what part we eat (second tithing), and what part we give to the needy stranger, fatherless and widows to eat (third tithing). Where do we draw the line between the part used in our homes and the part used in the house of God? You see why most preachers refer only to the Malachi version of tithe—because that is the passage they can easily use to cajole people. Pick any Bible version, carefully read all these passages, and then make up your mind based on facts.

Other passages about tithe in the scriptures are listed below:

And as soon as the commandment came abroad, the children of Israel brought in abundance the firstfruits of corn, wine, and oil, and honey, and of all the increase of the field; and the tithe of all things brought they in abundantly. And concerning the children of Israel and Judah, that dwelt in the cities of Judah, they also brought in the tithe of oxen and sheep, and the tithe of holy things which were consecrated unto the LORD their God, and laid them by heaps. (2 Chron, 31: 5-6 KJV)

And brought in the offerings and the tithes and the dedicated things faithfully: over which Cononiah the Levite was ruler, and Shimei his brother was the next. (2 Chron. 31:12 KJV)

And that we should bring the firstfruits of our dough, and our offerings, and the fruit of all manner of trees, of wine and of oil, unto the priests, to the chambers of the house of our God; and the tithes of our ground unto the Levites, that the same Levites might have the tithes in all the cities of our tillage. And the priest the son of Aaron shall be with the Levites, when the Levites take tithes: and the Levites shall bring up the tithe of the tithes unto the house of our God, to the chambers, into the treasure house. (Neh. 10:37-38 KJV)

And at that time were some appointed over the chambers for the treasures, for the offerings, for the firstfruits, and for the tithes, to gather into them out of the fields of the cities the portions of the law for the priests and Levites: for Judah rejoiced for the priests and for the Levites that waited. (Neh. 12:44 KJV)

And he had prepared for him a great chamber, where aforetime they laid the meat offerings, the frankincense, and the vessels, and the tithes of the corn, the new wine, and the oil, which was commanded to be given to the Levites, and the singers, and the porters; and the offerings of the priests. (Neh. 13:5 KJV)

Then brought all Judah the tithe of the corn and the new wine and the oil unto the treasuries. (Neh. 13:12 KJV)

Come to Bethel, and transgress; at Gilgal multiply transgression; and bring your sacrifices every morning, and your tithes after three years (Amos 4:4 KJV)

Nehemiah chapter 10 version brings new light. Tithe was paid in the rural towns. The only one that came to the temple was the tithe of tithes. This obviously is not what happens today. All tithes go to the headquarters.

Nehemiah chapter 12 version says tithe was given because the people loved the ministry. Can I love more than one ministry at a time? If yes, what do I do?

Nehemiah chapter 13 version says it also for the choir members and security guards.

The devilish doctrine today is to just bring your tithe; do not worry about what it is being used for. I cannot understand this doctrine. God did not just say, 'Bring your tithe.' He said, 'Bring your tithe for . . .' So why do I stop at bringing my tithe? If I pay my tithe, I must know that it is used for the purpose that tithe is meant to be used for; this is only scriptural. I must be sure it gets to the Levites, the widows, the fatherless, the strangers, the singers, and the gatekeepers. If I do not want to care about what it is being used for, I might as well just drop it by the roadside and walk away; after all, I have given my tithe.

We must definitely talk about one more passage. This is because it is about the only passage that most people know about tithe in the Bible. If you were to ask anyone about tithe, they would come straight to this passage. Everyone is afraid of a curse from the Lord. Our ministers have told us that if we do not pay tithe, we are under a curse. Let us follow this through systematically.

> *For I am the LORD, I change not; therefore ye sons of Jacob are not consumed. Even from the days of your fathers ye are gone away from mine ordinances, and have not kept them. Return unto me, and I will return unto you, saith the LORD of hosts. But ye said, Wherein shall we return? Will a man rob God? Yet ye have robbed me. But ye say, Wherein have we robbed thee? In tithes and offerings. Ye are cursed with a curse: for ye have robbed me, even this whole nation. Bring ye all the tithes into the storehouse, that there may be meat in mine house, and prove me now herewith, saith the LORD of hosts, if I will not open you the windows of heaven, and pour you out a blessing, that there shall not be room enough to receive it. And I will rebuke the devourer for your sakes, and he shall not destroy the fruits of your ground; neither shall your vine cast her fruit before the time in the field, saith the LORD of hosts. (Mal. 3:6-11 KJV)*

What is tithe? We have already seen that this is a most complex question to answer.

Who is to pay tithe? The sons of Jacob. This passage focused on the children of Israel, not Christians.

To whom is tithe paid? Here we are told to come drop it in the storehouse so that there will be food in the house for workers in the house. Even if we were to all pay tithes today, where is the house of God? I have heard preachers say it is the place where you worship. Can this be supported by the text of the scriptures putting in mind that not all tithes were brought to the storehouse; some were given to the poor, widows, and strangers, and part of tithe was eaten? They say this because there was only one temple in Israel at that time. Today there are many places of worship. Just as there are many banks, say ABC Bank. So if I want to give Mr. X money through the bank, does it matter where I pay it? If God is in Church Y and Church Z, and I decide to give it in Church Y, whereas I worship in Church Z, what is the problem? Am I giving to God or to man? You see how they lie over spiritual things they do not understand? Besides, we are all temples of God, so I can give to any person. I can also give to the poor. I can also eat my tithe. What happens to full-time workers who are not church members but in ministries not entirely a church organisation, like prison ministry, children welfare ministries, or NGO? Are they not doing God's work on a full-time basis? Should they not be compensated by the standard of the law of God? Why can't our ministers simply walk in sincerity and truth? Why are we using the pulpit to extort money?

What is the content of a tithe? The content is clear. Tithes of crops and animals: food in the house. We have seen that there were other professionals in Israel at that time. So this did not even apply to all the sons of Jacob!

What do you do with a tithe? It was for food in the temple for Levites and priest. It also includes food for the less privileged and the tithe payer from other passages above.

Other facts? This passage also mentions offerings. What was this offering? Was it money? Obviously, not in the context of this passage. Offering is meat offering, sin offering, guilt offering, and so forth—blood of lambs and bulls that could not cleanse sin. Why are we not bringing that to God as well? Offerings can now be other monies you give. Rubbish! It is either blood or not. You cannot give money. Without the shedding of blood, there is no remission of sin.

Jesus also said something about tithing to the Pharisees:

> The Lord said to him, "You Pharisees clean the outside of the cup and the dish. But inside you are full of greed and evil. You are foolish. The same One who made what is outside also made what is inside. So give what is in your cups and dishes to the poor. Then you will be fully clean. But how terrible for you Pharisees! You give God one-tenth of even your mint, your rue, and every other plant in your garden. But you forget to be fair to other people and to love God. These are the things you should do. And you should also continue to do those other things—like giving one-tenth. How terrible for you Pharisees, because you love to get the most important seats in the synagogues. And you love people to show respect to you in the marketplaces. How terrible for you, because you are like hidden graves. People walk on them without knowing it." (Luke 11:39-44 ICB)

Who pays tithe? Here Jesus is talking to the Pharisee, not his disciple. The new covenant was yet to start. Even these religious people still made mistakes with tithing. How do we think we can go back to tithing and not miss it? You hear that tithe should be before tax; no, it should be after tax. It should be the increase or profit. What is my salary, net or gross? Confusion? Do you really think you can beat the Pharisees in laws of tithing? Before the new covenant started by the death of Jesus, which is the fulfilment of all the laws, Jesus warned that we should concentrate more on the things of mercy and judgement. These are weightier things of the law. Do you know that when the apostles tried to draft a law for the new convert Gentiles, they made no mention of anything other than idol worship? These people were with Jesus. They concentrated on the other weightier things of the law.

What is the content of tithe? The content of tithes here referred to again by Jesus is not money, just plants.

> *'I give up eating twice a week, and I give one-tenth of everything I earn!'*
> *The tax collector stood at a distance. When he prayed, he would not*
> *even look up to heaven. He beat on his chest because he was so sad.*
> *He said, 'God, have mercy on me. I am a sinner!' I tell you, when*
> *this man went home, he was right with God. But the Pharisee was*
> *not right with God. Everyone who makes himself great will be made*
> *humble. But everyone who makes himself humble will be made great.*
> (Luke 18:12-14 ICB)

Jesus said there is this tendency for a man to think that blessings and forgiveness come from work. No, they do not. They come by grace and grace alone. God shows us mercy not because we merit it. It is interesting to note here that in the passage above, Jesus was careful not to add giving to the poor as part of what the Pharisee did, for in His preaching He had said that if you give a cup of cold water to a little child you will not lose your reward. We cannot go back to such an unclear doctrine in the scripture that Jesus technically cancelled.

- We do not know what tithe is.
- We do not know what per cent it is.
- We do not know who to pay it to.
- We do not know the content.
- We do not know what to use it for.

There are so many more questions on tithe that cannot be answered clearly. Romans 13 says that the people in government are God's ministers. So why can I not give them my tithes?

> *All of you must obey the government rulers. No one rules unless God*
> *has given him the power to rule. And no one rules now without that*
> *power from God. So if anyone is against the government, he is really*
> *against what God has commanded. And so he brings punishment on*
> *himself. Those who do right do not have to fear the rulers. But people*
> *who do wrong must fear them. Do you want to be unafraid of the*
> *rulers? Then do what is right, and the ruler will praise you. He is*

> *God's servant to help you. But if you do wrong, then be afraid. The ruler has the power to punish; he is God's servant to punish those who do wrong.* (Rom. 13:1-4 ICB)

Irrefutably, in the entire scriptures, one thing is clear: we must honour God with our income. We must set apart our money to honour God. If you are methodical and set it as a percentage (say 1 per cent, 10 per cent, or 100 per cent), that is okay. If you decide to give as needed, that is okay. We cannot own all we earn. We must care for the poor, the needy, the widows, the strangers, and so forth. This is what I think the passages below mean.

> *You will harvest your crops on your land. But do not harvest all the way to the corners of your field. If grain falls onto the ground, don't gather it up. Leave it for poor people and foreigners in your country. I am the Lord your God.* (Lev. 23:22 ICB)

> *If you ignore the poor when they cry for help, you also will cry for help and not be answered.* (Prov. 21:13 ICB)

> *If a person asks you for something, then give it to him. Don't refuse to give to a person who wants to borrow from you.* (Matt. 5:42 ICB)

It is a sin for you to eat 100 per cent of what you earn because along the line, you would have broken the spirit of these passages. All across the Bible, one fact remains clear: care for humanity.

So we do not get things confused, we shall look at Jesus' ministry on Earth. Did he take tithes from people? How did He run His ministry?

2.4   *Giving alms and offerings: Jesus and early church era*

> And he touched her hand, and the fever left her: and she arose, and ministered unto them. (Matt. 8:15 KJV)

This passage gives insight to the type of life Jesus led while on earth. Indeed, this is the kind of life we, as ministers, are all supposed to live—one day at a time. We are told here that Jesus performed a miracle and the woman was able to prepare food for them. Foxes indeed have holes and birds have nests; the Son of Man had nowhere to lay His head. Ministers should emulate this. You cannot want the things that are spiritual and still want to have the things that are physical. Paul said that if you are single, you are concerned only with the things of God. While I am not trying to preach that people should not marry, I would like to say that people should count the cost before they say they want to be ministers. We can consider being a part-time minister like Paul, one of the greatest ministers. This way, money matters in the church will be easier. We should decide where we want our reward: heaven or earth. If we are really doing spiritual service, then let us wait for our reward in heaven. If it is for money, why are we pretending it is spiritual?

In this passage, we see an example of the New Testament giving. There is a need and the grateful provided to meet the need. Once you have the strength and the means, please meet the need. This is out of thanksgiving. Indeed, all our giving should be out of thanksgiving. It would have been strange if the woman practised what is preached today in the church: 'Give your seed an assignment.' How do you think this would have been? The woman stands before Jesus and says, 'I am giving this food because I am believing you for . . .' I am almost sure Jesus would have turned some stones into bread rather than eat her food. She gave her food to Jesus. *Period.* This should be our example: just give and satisfy the need. Give out of a grateful heart. We cannot say whether her giving was 10 per cent or more or less. This is the New Testament giving. She was giving directly to Jesus, who owes tithes and offerings in the first case.

Another example is given below:

> *Many women were standing at a distance from the cross, watching. These were women who had followed Jesus from Galilee to care for him.* (Matt. 27:55 ICB)

Some women were standing at a distance from the cross, watching. Some of these women were Mary Magdalene, Salome, and Mary the mother of James and Joseph. (James was her youngest son.) These were the women who followed Jesus in Galilee and cared for him. Many other women were also there who had come with Jesus to Jerusalem. (Mark 15:40-41 ICB)

There were also some women with him who had been healed of sicknesses and evil spirits. One of the women was Mary, called Magdalene, from whom seven demons had gone out. Also among the women were Joanna, the wife of Chuza (Herod's helper), Susanna, and many other women. These women used their own money to help Jesus and his apostles. (Luke 8:2-3 ICB)

Some people had had some encounters with Jesus; they were contributing from their private purse to the support of Jesus and his disciples. We even read of a wife of a servant to King Herod. Jesus was not just using government money here! These people were all born again. Mind you, they found no fault in Him. Only those people who had been saved gave to Jesus. We should not allow bad money into the church. No one must offer a cursed thing to the Lord. We are again not told what percentage of the income they gave. They gave. *Period.* They gave to satisfy the need of Jesus. Everything we own belongs to God. If he needs 10 per cent, give. If he needs 100 per cent, give. Give as you see the need. Let us look at what the apostle Paul says:

You know that I always worked to take care of my own needs and the needs of those who were with me. I showed you in all things that you should work as I did and help the weak. I taught you to remember the words of Jesus. He said, 'It is more blessed to give than to receive.' (Acts 20:34-35 ICB)

The minister (Paul) in this case is the one living by example. He is the one leading the movement. By his living, he is showing that he would rather give than receive. He was ministering and feeding himself outside the ministry. Why do we think every minister must eat from the church today? Why do you think you must eat from your book, music, or tape? The example we have of Paul here is that he was ministering and he had another source of income. Was he less efficient? Maybe by his own standard, surely not by our standards, for no one is doing what he has done. This is the same man whose personal letter to a friend (Philemon) is kept in the Bible as the word of God. We need to be able to differentiate career from calling. Many people are doing what will put bread on the table, yet they want us to feel that they are doing it for God. Were you successful by all standards in what you were doing before you were called to the ministry? The disciples were not idle before they were called. Do you have the education, skills, or experience to engage in any other work to earn money? It is more blessed to give money than to receive money. We have many lazy and idle hands claiming they are in the ministry when in fact they are looking for daily bread. I have no problem with them if they will just own up to the fact that they are singing in the church as a job. Let them not be claiming they are doing God's work. Do not pray and say that God should speak through you and then go ahead and sell the tape and pocket the money. You are stealing directly from God. Look at the ministers you know: the ones that were at the peak of their careers when they laid it down and said, 'I want to be poor,' and the ones that were nobody and said that they want to be ministers. You will see two distinct groups: the greedy ministers and the ministers that are content with what they have. Why do we preach money, money, money today in the church? Hebrews 11:36-38 also says that by faith, some became destitute. What are we doing with the money? Look at the passage below:

> Now I am going to Jerusalem to help God's people. The believers in Macedonia and Southern Greece were happy to give their money to help the poor among God's people at Jerusalem. (Rom. 15:25-26 ICB)

We see here that there was an offering given by these Christians to help poor Christians in Jerusalem. At this time, some of the apostles were still in Jerusalem. They were poor and needed help. This is another instance of money (or goods) in the early church. The aim was to help needy Christians. Why are we not part of this today as Christians? Christianity is a movement that must retain its cutting edge. We do not know why times were hard—maybe famine, maybe persecution, maybe some other reasons. There are so many Christians today in different countries suffering for many reasons. Do we not think that Christianity would be more powerful if we would give to support these needy ones? We need these kinds of offerings. Sometimes when we put money in the offering basket as it passes by in the church service, I wonder if it is just a routine or if it is for a particular project. I also wonder when it is said to be for a particular project whether it will all be used for the project. God will help us all. We cannot assume it is for the welfare of church workers, as stated below.

> *Surely you know that those who work at the Temple get their food from the Temple. And those who serve at the altar get part of what is offered at the altar. It is the same with those who tell the Good News. The Lord has commanded that those who tell the Good News should get their living from this work.* (1 Cor. 9:13-14 ICB)

Every church clinches to this verse, stating that those who preach the gospel should eat by the gospel. I have no problem at all with that. It may be a universal principle. However, we should ask a few pragmatic questions. Are they really preaching the good news? How many times in a year do they make altar calls for people to give their lives to Jesus? If they are paid by the church for doing the job of preaching, why do they double-dip by selling their tapes and books? Are there not people like Paul (who wrote this), who despite this, worked for their money without touching the church purse? Let me give three classes of Christians, indeed three classes of ministers.

There are those who preach for what they can get here on Earth. These are the prosperity people. Their message: Give and you will be given, and you will not lose your reward here on earth. I must say that they are at the lowest state of Christianity. They are the kind of crowd that was looking for Jesus because he fed them. Listen to the kind of conversation, or prayer, these people have with God every day:

> *Jesus replied, "The truth of the matter is that you want to be with me because I fed you, not because you believe in me. But you shouldn't be so concerned about perishable things like food. No, spend your*

energy seeking the eternal life that I, the Messiah, can give you. For
God the Father has sent me for this very purpose."
They replied, "What should we do to satisfy God?"
Jesus told them, "This is the will of God, that you believe in the
one he has sent."
They replied, "You must show us more miracles if you want us to
believe you are the Messiah. Give us free bread every day, like our
fathers had while they journeyed through the wilderness! As the
Scriptures say, 'Moses gave them bread from heaven.'"
Jesus said, "Moses didn't give it to them. My Father did. And
now he offers you true Bread from heaven. The true Bread is a
Person—the one sent by God from heaven, and he gives life to the
world."
"Sir," they said, "give us that bread every day of our lives!"
Jesus replied, "I am the Bread of Life. No one coming to me will
ever be hungry again. Those believing in me will never thirst. (John
6:26-34 TLB)

The second class of Christians believe their reward is in heaven: this is
where normal Christians belong. They are willing to become destitute
because of the gospel. Their focus is in heaven. They have the 'work
and pay' mentality. Their payment is in heaven. They are prepared to
wait. This is the middle part.

We have the peak of Christianity. Here Christians just click into the
very mind of God, the very kingdom of God. All they want is that
the work of God be done. They key into the essence of the war of the
universe: God versus Satan, good versus evil. They are willing to lay
down their lives for the victory of His kingdom. Here on earth they
do not want anything. In the world to come, they are ready to lose.
All they want is for God to win the war: people must be saved. Think
of Moses, who said, 'Your work must be done.' People must be saved
even if it means blotting my own name away. Listen to Moses.

So Moses went back to the Lord and said, "How terrible it is! These
people have sinned horribly. They have made for themselves gods
from gold. Now, forgive them of this sin. If you will not, then erase

my name. Erase it from the book in which you have written the names of your people."
But the Lord told Moses, "I will erase from my book the names of the people who sin against me. (Exod. 32:31-33 ICB)

Paul also said:

I am in Christ, and I am telling you the truth. I do not lie. My feelings are ruled by the Holy Spirit, and they tell me that I am not lying. I have great sorrow and always feel much sadness for the Jewish people. I wish I could help my Jewish brothers, my people. I would even wish that I were cursed and cut off from Christ if that would help them. (Rom. 9:1-3 ICB)

Side by side, we do not match Paul. Yet all his labour on Earth he lost: for by faith, he died a wretched man. All his labour in heaven he was ready to lose for people to be saved. Indeed, these people are entitled to eat from the gospel not our modern preachers who are not interested in salvation of souls. Here again is another example:

You know that the family of Stephanas were the first believers in Southern Greece. They have given themselves to the service of God's people. I ask you, brothers, to follow the leading of people like these and anyone else who works and serves with them. (1 Cor. 16:15-16 ICB)

Christians like these are few. Everyone is talking about how you can have breakthroughs and prosperity. For the past twenty to thirty years, that has been the theme of every year. Here we have the family of Stephanas, who knew what responsibility was upon them as the first believers; they spent their lives helping and serving other Christians everywhere. Were these people concerned with years of open doors and years of favour? The Holy Ghost says we can only listen to these people and people like them who work so hard with real devotion. Do you see why that entire seminar, symposium, motivational speakers' conference, and so forth, cannot be for you? Listen to people who are sincerely devoted to helping others in need. Follow these people. Hear these people. Let us look at another example, this time of a church:

But they asked us again and again—they begged us to let them share
in this service for God's people. And they gave in a way that we did
not expect: They first gave themselves to the Lord and to us. This is
what God wants. (2 Cor. 8:4-5 ICB)

This church knew what was important: helping humanity. They
begged for it. What does the church beg for today? Media, publicity,
promotions, and so forth. Let us pause here and ask ourselves questions.
Consider how much we spend for advertisements on TV. If we spend
our money as a church helping the poor, the TV will come to us,
the radios will come to us, and newspapers will come to us, as it will
help with their adverts and promotions. How much liquid money
transactions did Jesus made? Jesus' self recognition was enough for
the owner of the colt to let it go when Jesus needed to ride one
into Jerusalem. If the church does the right thing, companies will be
clothing ministers, furnishing our churches, buying all our gadgets,
printing our books—in short, everything will be done for free for us.
Why do I think so? These companies want to advertise; they want to
sell their products. So I find it difficult to understand when people say,
'The church needs money.' I know that what we need are believers.
Many things we spend money on as a church, we can get for free. Do
we not hear of celebrities (I still wonder why we have to celebrate
them) threatening to get court orders to keep the media away from
them? The church should just do the right things. While some people
are tired of media, the church is paying so much to get them.

Here again is another example of the church.

I really do not need to write to you about this help for God's people.
I know that you want to help. I have been bragging about this to the
people in Macedonia. I have told them that you in Southern Greece
have been ready to give since last year. And your wanting to give has
made most of them here ready to give also. But I am sending the
brothers to you. I do not want our bragging about you in this to be
for nothing. I want you to be ready, as I said you would be. If any
of the people from Macedonia come with me and find that you are
not ready, we will be ashamed. We will be ashamed that we were
so sure of you. [And you will be ashamed too!] So I thought that

I should ask these brothers to go to you before we come. They will finish getting in order the gift you promised. Then the gift will be ready when we come, and it will be a gift you wanted to give—not a gift that you hated to give. Remember this: The person who plants a little will have a small harvest. But the person who plants a lot will have a big harvest. Each one should give, then, what he has decided in his heart to give. He should not give if it makes him sad. And he should not give if he thinks he is forced to give. God loves the person who gives happily. And God can give you more blessings than you need. Then you will always have plenty of everything. You will have enough to give to every good work. It is written in the Scriptures: "He gives freely to the poor. The things he does are right and will continue forever." (2 Cor. 9:1-15 ICB)

God is the One who gives seed to the farmer. And he gives bread for food. And God will give you all the seed you need and make it grow. He will make a great harvest from your goodness. God will make you rich in every way so that you can always give freely. And your giving through us will cause many to give thanks to God. This service that you do helps the needs of God's people. It is also bringing more and more thanks to God. This service you do is a proof of your faith. Many people will praise God because of it. They will praise God because you follow the Good News of Christ—the gospel you say you believe. They will praise God because you freely share with them and with all others. And when they pray, they will wish they could be with you. They will feel this because of the great grace that God has given you. Thanks be to God for his gift that is too wonderful to explain. (Psalm 112:9-15 ICB)

Again, we see here that giving was to help people. The church should help all needy saints. This would make people, including TV, to glorify God. As we help humanity, God too will help us.

God is fair. He will not forget the work you did and the love you showed for him by helping his people. And he will remember that you are still helping them. (Heb. 6:10 ICB)

What I do not understand today is why money in the church is used for ministers to stay in five-star hotels and even own private planes, while people in church are suffering and cannot boast of a good meal in a day. Why are our schools not free for the needy? I cannot imagine the man who is supposedly leading us to war being entangled by the affairs of this world. Yet he tells me to set my affections on things above. The love described here is the love shown to God by helping His people. When you stand to pray and say that you love the Lord, remember that your love for God, whom you do not see, is measured by the love for people that you see. The book of James says the summary of religion is to provide for the needy and keep yourself pure. How best can I love God other than giving him my offering and tithe through giving to other people? Paul would say to do good to everyone, especially those of the household of faith.

> Jesus answered, "If you want to be perfect, then go and sell all the things you own. Give the money to the poor. If you do this, you will have a treasure in heaven. Then come and follow me!" But when the young man heard this, he became very sad because he was very rich. So he left Jesus. (Matt. 19:21-22 ICB)

If only people would, like this young man, leave Jesus alone. The young man knew he could not do what he was being asked to do, so he left Jesus. He may have been sad. It may have been a sad thing, indeed a soul may have been lost, yet he went away. He left Jesus alone. Ministers and all sort of ministers should make up their minds, count the cost, and leave Him alone. You cannot serve God and mammon. You cannot have your mind set on the things of this world and still have treasures in heaven. Jesus said to detach yourself from the things of this world. Sell all you have. Let the only thing that matters be the kingdom of God. The Bible says if we must be perfect, we must sell all that we have. Some people have been arguing whether if it is money or the love of money that is the root of evil over the years, and whether the rich will go to hell fire. Jesus said that it is extremely hard. Except this is not what was said. Why do we not use the same acid test today: how much are you detached from what you have?

It is surprising that nearly all we hear in the church today are messages about money and prosperity. Is it not worthy of note that though Jesus corrected this rich young man about calling people good, He did not correct him when he said he has kept the laws from when he was young? Among the laws were tithe and offering laws, which we clamour about today. He needed to be perfect by selling all he had, detaching himself from the world and money and following Jesus. You cannot follow Jesus without first detaching yourself. Wrangling and breakups in the church could be reduced if we detached ourselves from money and self.

We see that the counsel from Jesus was clear: sell and give to the poor. Strangely, this is very different from the message from the altar today. Today's message is bring to the church. Bring to the ministers. Do we not see the difference? The young man did not see Jesus as a con man. Jesus needed resources, so to speak, for His ministry. By buying horses and chariots for travel, he would have been able to reach all those Jews who were already scattered abroad. The church needs money, as some claim. Yet Jesus told the man to give to the poor. Where is the best place to be sure that your good work is stored in heaven when you give? Give to the poor. Why are we not preaching to give to the poor today? Ministers want the money. Why are we singing to make money and calling it ministry? Why are we writing books to make money and calling it ministry? Why are we setting up schools to make money and calling it ministry? How can it be ministry if it is profiteering? Ministers today want personal money. Many people today see ministers as con men. Does that not bother us? I suppose it should. Does the Bible not say we should not let people shame the name of God? Do we ever think about what goes on in the hearts of TV viewers when we stand at the altar calling for all sorts of seed offerings? The name of our God is blasphemed for our sake. God forgive us. We do not care about the source of money. All we want is seed offering, miracle seed, and covenant sowing. We call it all sorts of names.

Let us look at some more examples of Jesus:

While Jesus was there, a woman came to him. She had an alabaster jar filled with expensive perfume. She poured this perfume on Jesus' head while he was eating. His followers saw the woman do this and were upset. They asked, "Why waste that perfume? It could be sold for a great deal of money, and the money could be given to the poor." But Jesus knew what happened. He said, "Why are you troubling this woman? She did a very beautiful thing for me. You will always have the poor with you. But you will not always have me. This woman poured perfume on my body to prepare me for burial. I tell you the truth. The Good News will be told to people in all the world. And in every place where it is preached, what this woman has done will be told. And people will remember her." (Matt. 26:7-13 ICB)

But Zacchaeus said to the Lord, "I will give half of my money to the poor. If I have cheated anyone, I will pay that person back four times more!" Jesus said, "Salvation has come to this house today. This man truly belongs to the family of Abraham. The Son of Man came to find lost people and save them." (Luke 19:8-10 ICB)

Again, here we have issues about money during the time of Jesus. I once was talking about bad money in the church to a minister, and he cited this, as Jesus accepting money made from prostitution, to tell me not to be concerned about the source of money in the church. I must say that I was shocked. Yes, the money may have been from prostitution, but it was not from a prostitute. She had repented. This indeed is a story of repentance and being born again, which we hear about in the scriptures—the power of the gospel. A songwriter says, 'Things I used to love, I love them no more'. The woman used to love money, and she did all sorts of things to get it. She gave that same wealth to Jesus when she became a changed person. Her heart was already accepted before her offering. She gave that which all her life she had toiled for and sold her body for. This money was restitution to God. She had almost destroyed her body, which was not hers. Are you surprised that indeed this money does not belong to the poor? It must be given to the giver of life. How can we call this bad money? How can we say that we as ministers should not be concerned about the souls and indeed the source of the money giver? When we as ministers call for whatever name we have coined for the offering, do we care what the source of the money is?

This is about the same lesson from the story of Zacchaeus. When he was disconnected from the bondage of love for money, Jesus said this was a sign that salvation has come into the home. The sign that you are saved—or do we say one of the signs?—is that you are detached from money and the love of it. Zacchaeus had oppressed and taken what was not due him. He wanted money. Love for money, indeed. It does not matter whose head you climbed as a ladder. When salvation came and truly a heart of stone was changed to a heart of flesh, he gave 50 per cent of the money to the poor first of all. Then he was ready to give 400 per cent to anyone he had cheated from the rest of the 50 per cent. My God! This is indeed the power of the gospel. This was restitution to the people he cheated. He did not say, 'I give Jesus half of the goods,' as many ministers would encourage us to do today. He suddenly saw God not only in his heart but in his house. God helps us to have this glimpse of His glory. Jesus said this is a sign that salvation has come into this house. Bad money again from a good man. This is the only money we can accept in His church, indeed the only money God accepts. You cannot bring money got from evil ways to the church. It must be without blemish. Peter asked Ananias if what he received was the whole money from the land that Ananias sold. Peter knew the source of the money. We may not be able to know the source of every penny in the church, but we must preach that bad money cannot be accepted by our God.

Were this woman and this man sowing seed? Were they giving and praying over their offerings? "God, as I give to the poor, you fill my barn . . ." No. they were just detached. God will help us all. Why are we turning the church into eating and drinking? The kingdom of God should not be meat and drink.

> *In the kingdom of God, eating and drinking are not important. The important things are living right with God, peace, and joy in the Holy Spirit. Anyone who serves Christ by living this way is pleasing God and will be accepted by other people. (Rom. 14:17-18 ICB)*

Over the last years, we are so concerned with messages of breakthroughs and open doors that we are losing the cutting edge of Christianity. I wonder if this is not a direct disregard of Jesus' words.

Jesus said to his followers, "So I tell you, don't worry about the food you need to live. Don't worry about the clothes you need for your body. Life is more important than food. And the body is more important than clothes. Look at the birds. They don't plant or harvest. They don't save food in houses or barns. But God takes care of them. And you are worth much more than birds. None of you can add any time to your life by worrying about it. If you cannot do even the little things, then why worry about the big things? Look at the wild flowers. See how they grow. They don't work or make clothes for themselves. But I tell you that even Solomon, the great and rich king, was not dressed as beautifully as one of these flowers. God clothes the grass in the field like that. That grass is living today, but tomorrow it will be thrown into the fire. So you know how much more God will clothe you. Don't have so little faith! Don't always think about what you will eat or what you will drink. Don't worry about it. All the people in the world are trying to get those things. Your Father knows that you need them. The thing you should seek is God's kingdom. Then all the other things you need will be given to you. Don't fear, little flock. Your Father wants to give you the kingdom. Sell the things you have and give to the poor. Get for yourselves purses that don't wear out. Get the treasure in heaven that never runs out. Thieves can't steal it in heaven, and moths can't destroy it. Your heart will be where your treasure is." (Luke 12:22-34 ICB)

I have met many people who have asked me how ministers would eat if they did not sell their books or tapes. I get worried because we have missed it. Who is a minister? The leader. The commander of God's army. Here Jesus says all his soldiers should not seek what to eat or what to drink. Here is a minister who is the leader of mission. If he does not want to be a minister, let him go and work. If he is a minister, let him count the cost. It is that simple. Take the example of Peter:

But Peter said, "I don't have any silver or gold, but I do have something else I can give you: By the power of Jesus Christ from Nazareth—stand up and walk!" (Acts 3:6 ICB)

Was Peter lying about not having silver and gold? I do not think so. We have seen ministers of the gospel pursue so much silver and gold, yet what they are supposed to have, they no longer have. We no longer fear God, like Simon in the story below.

> *Simon saw that the Spirit was given to people when the apostles laid their hands on them. So he offered the apostles money. He said, "Give me also this power so that when I lay my hands on a person, he will receive the Holy Spirit." Peter said to him, "You and your money should both be destroyed! You thought you could buy God's gift with money. You cannot share with us in this work. Your heart is not right before God. Change your heart! Turn away from this evil thing you have done. Pray to the Lord. Maybe he will forgive you for thinking this. I see that you are full of bitter jealousy and ruled by sin." (Acts 8:18-23 ICB)*

The Bible says of Cornelius that he was a devout man, one who feared God. Then he gave alms to the people. The order cannot be reversed. It has always been the giver before the gift. It is disheartening what we hear in churches today. It is more like give, sow a seed, and bring your money, buying the gifts and blessing of God with it. They come in different forms: three-day miracle seed, twenty-four-hour miracle seed, and so on. The ministers paint an image that once you give, you have made a covenant with God and He will bless you. You cannot buy His blessings with money. Who tells you that God is interested in entering a covenant with you? Why do we preach money as if it is the only way to receive from God? We select the passages in the Bible and quote some parts in the scriptures, leaving the rest. As ministers, we do not follow passages like the one below.

> *When I was with you, I never wanted anyone's money or fine clothes. You know that I always worked to take care of my own needs and the needs of those who were with me. I showed you in all things that you should work as I did and help the weak. I taught you to remember the words of Jesus. He said, 'It is more blessed to give than to receive.'* (Acts 20:33-35 ICB)

This verse is rarely heard from the pulpit. If you are a minister and you can boldly say, like Paul, that your hands have worked to pay your own way and even to supply the needs of those who are with you, then you are among the few. Few people are preaching like Paul today. How many are writing books for free today? Why are those who do not depend on church money so few? When you hear that it is more blessed to give than to receive, it almost does not include the minister. From this verse alone, we can say that ministers should all go and work for their upkeep. Ministers should develop skills and work. We cannot pretend we are ministering when all we are doing is making money. I wonder how we can record our messages and songs, then sell the tapes or CD, enrich ourselves and yet claim we are ministering in God's name. At the end of the day, we are not storing up in heaven when we are already receiving our reward here on earth. I honestly hope that I am wrong in my line of thought—because if by some chance I am right, heaven indeed will not have any of the familiar faces we see here on Earth.

The instructions from the scriptures are clear enough:

> *Love each other like brothers and sisters. Give your brothers and sisters more honor than you want for yourselves. Do not be lazy but work hard. Serve the Lord with all your heart. Be joyful because you have hope. Be patient when trouble comes. Pray at all times. Share with God's people who need help. Bring strangers in need into your homes.* (Rom. 12:10-13 ICB)

Are these verses not glaring instructions on what the church should do with money? The church should be in the habit of helping God's children in need. Can our roles in this world be clearer than this? Anytime I see castles (churches) being converted to pubs, warehouses, and the like, my heart groans. If the money was actually used to build lives rather than buildings, I wonder what the result would have been today. We removed God from the buildings; therefore, the buildings are useless for spiritual matters. The same way we are building schools and monuments with God's money today, yet God is not there. Our role is to champion poverty eradication first from God's children and then from the world. Oh, I know the Bible says that we will always have the poor. That is even more reason why we know this task is eternal. There is always work to be done.

Consider this interesting passage in the Bible:

> *Now I will write about the collection of money for God's people. Do the same thing that I told the Galatian churches to do: On the first day of every week, each one of you should put aside as much money as you can from what you are blessed with. You should save it up, so that you will not have to collect money after I come. When I arrive, I will send some men to take your gift to Jerusalem. These will be men who you all agree should go. I will send them with letters of introduction. If it seems good for me to go also, these men will go along with me.* (1 Cor. 16:1-4 ICB)

I guess these are the Sunday offerings we make today. We see clearly why the offerings were made: for the saints in Jerusalem. Saints who were suffering. Am I saying all offerings must be for the poor? No! As we see here, there was a need, and people gave. They all knew why they were giving. If you want to buy public address systems in the church, just say so. Why are you going through three-day miracle seed and twenty-four-hour glory sowing? Tell the people what is needed. Let them give and account for the money afterwards. But it is of great importance that this money was for the poor. When people are genuinely born again, they will give. When we give to those in need, then our faith is not dead.

> *And you say to him, "God be with you! I hope you stay warm and get plenty to eat." You say this, but you do not give that person the things he needs. Unless you help him, your words are worth nothing. It is the same with faith. If faith does nothing, then that faith is dead, because it is alone.* (James 2:16-17 ICB)

While we know we should help our teachers by paying them, as stated below, the teachers must define why they are teaching.

> *Anyone who is learning the teaching of God should share all the good things he has with his teacher.* (Gala. 6 ICB)

The question is, why is the teacher teaching? Why is the minister ministering? When Paul got gifts from the Philippians church, he said, 'Thank you, but I really did not seek it.'

> You people in Philippi remember when I first preached the Good News there. When I left Macedonia, you were the only church that gave me help. Several times you sent me things I needed when I was in Thessalonica. Really, it is not that I want to receive gifts from you. But I want you to have the good that comes from giving. And now I have everything, and more. I have all I need because Epaphroditus brought your gift to me. Your gift is like a sweet-smelling sacrifice offered to God. God accepts that sacrifice, and it pleases him. My God will use his wonderful riches in Christ Jesus to give you everything you need. (Phil. 4:15-19 ICB)

Paul said to let the rich give. He also said not to forget to give.

> Give this command to those who are rich with things of this world. Tell them not to be proud. Tell them to hope in God, not their money. Money cannot be trusted, but God takes care of us richly. He gives us everything to enjoy. Tell the rich people to do good and to be rich in doing good deeds. Tell them to be happy to give and ready to share. By doing that, they will be saving a treasure for themselves in heaven. That treasure will be a strong foundation. Their future life can be built on that treasure. Then they will be able to have the life that is true life. (1 Tim. 6:17-19 ICB)

> Do not forget to do good to others. And share with them what you have. These are the sacrifices that please God. (Heb. 13:16 ICB)

Here is the verse that most ministers quote to get money from people. Please read it carefully.

> "Don't judge other people, and you will not be judged. Don't accuse others of being guilty, and you will not be accused of being guilty. Forgive other people, and you will be forgiven. Give, and you will receive. You will be given much. It will be poured into your hands—more than you can hold. You will be given so much that it

will spill into your lap. The way you give to others is the way God will give to you." (Luke 6:37–38 ICB)

Does it not jump out almost immediately that though we can apply it to money, it is not fundamentally referring to money? This passage simply refers to the way we relate with others. If you set a standard for others, they will set a higher standard for you. Yet they quote this verse to get money from people.

2.5   Vows

I do not understand how vows came into the church of today. They call it all sorts of names: seed, seed of faith, prosperity seed, and so forth.

There are only two references to vows in the New Testament: Acts 18:18 and Acts 21: 23. Both of them are related to the Nazarene vow. Are we supposed to keep this? No.

This is one bit that I find very difficult in the church today. We all need to wake up! I do not think we have an example of Jesus Christ to follow in this case. I cannot recall any account about Him making a vow.

What is a vow? A promise made, in our case, to God! I do not intend to dwell much on this at all. It is a slippery path that the church must not walk. Maybe we should look at some promises to God that men made in the past.

> And then Jacob saw the Lord standing above the ladder. The Lord said, "I am the Lord, the God of Abraham, your grandfather. And I am the God of Isaac. I will give you and your descendants the land on which you are now sleeping. Your descendants will be as many as the dust of the earth. They will spread west and east, north and south. All the families of the earth will be blessed through you and your descendants. I am with you, and I will protect you everywhere you go. And I will bring you back to this land. I will not leave you until I have done what I have promised you."

Then Jacob woke from his sleep. He said, "Surely the Lord is in this place. But I did not know it." Jacob was afraid. He said, "This place frightens me! It is surely the house of God and the gate of heaven." Jacob rose early in the morning. He took the stone he had slept on and set it up on its end. Then he poured olive oil on the top of it. At first, the name of that city was Luz. But Jacob named it Bethel. Then Jacob made a promise. He said, "I want God to be with me and protect me on this journey. I want God to give me food to eat and clothes to wear. Then I will be able to return in peace to my father's house. If the Lord does these things, he will be my God. This stone which I have set up on its end will be the house of God. And I will give God one-tenth of all he gives me." (Gen. 28:13–22 ICB)

God told Jacob, "I will be with you." Jacob said, "If you will be with me". Jacob was lucky he was not dealing with angel Gabriel. The response would have been, 'I am saying I will be with you . . . You will be dumb until . . .' He woke up and was like, 'God is in this place?' Which place? The place he slept! Had he lain down some couple of yards away, what would have happened? It would have been another place that God was. We as humans can be very superstitious. Then in this same irrational manner, he made an unnecessary vow instead of just saying, 'Thank you, Lord.' There is no record in the Bible that he fulfilled his vow. I am not saying that he did not. We just do not have it recorded. Do you know that this vow would have haunted him for almost about twenty-one years (seven years for Leah and seven years for Rachel—about seven years of working Laban for wages)? The tithe matter was at best a personal promise. This is what today's preachers want us to emulate. What role did this vow play in what God wanted to do? Is God not more interested in obedience rather than sacrifice anymore? Why do we preach this vow as if we can drag God into a covenant by ourselves? It takes two to agree. God has already said come unto me, 'I will give you rest.' So why do you think you can buy the things of God with money? Peter said, 'Your money perishes with you . . .' God has a programme you cannot change. If you like, pray like Paul three times, and all you will hear is that my grace is sufficient. If you were to meet Jesus today, he would tell you, 'Go and sell all you have; give it to the poor and then come and follow me.' He is not interested in your money. The only thing that He is interested in is your serving him with all your heart. That is all. This is what is missing in the church today. When God revisited this vow in Genesis 31:13, He told Jacob, 'Where you made a vow ...' Not where *we* made a vow. It was Jacob, not God and Jacob. God has never clouded His intent concerning His desire: He has regards for you, and afterward He has regards for your offering. Remember Cain and Abel.

Let us look at another vow in Chapter 6 in the book of Numbers. This was voluntary. It was for any man or woman who wants to serve God in a special way as an Israelite. This is the only reflected upon in the Acts of the apostle by Paul. It is part of the laws of Moses. Today we should all promise to serve God to the end. It has nothing to do with money.

What is the vow and promise we make today? Let us realise that all we need is to serve God. All we have is for God. If He needs it, we give. Do not let anyone push you into making a promise you cannot keep. If there is a need in the church, do what you can at that time, not because you want to blackmail God into doing something for you. Do it because there is a need.

2.6　Conclusion

Tithe is Old Testament stuff we do not understand so well. Tithe was only for crops and animals, not money. There were people who were not farmers in Israel. When he referred to tithing, Jesus did not condemn it, but do not forget that the new covenant had not started. We have no record of the apostles paying tithes. If you want to pay tithe, then go back to all the laws in the Old Testament. You do not gain anything from God because of works. It is by grace. To go back to the law, your righteousness must exceed that of the Pharisee. I advise you not to go down this way; Jesus, who made the statement below, is the judge on the last day, and there is no appeal.

> *I tell you that you must do better than the teachers of the law and the Pharisees. If you are not better than they are, you will not enter the kingdom of heaven.* (Matt. 5:20 ICB)

We saw that despite the short ministry, Jesus had enough and had an account for the poor. We also looked at how the early church survived.

As a child in the Sunday school, I always heard the story of how Noah built the ark. As I grew up, many questions filled my mind about the story. This ark was a massive one, well beyond its era. How did he build it? This man, moved by fear, engaged in this mega project. Let us pause as ministers and weigh our lives again. Are we not ashamed knowing we are encompassed by these great crowds of witnesses? Do we really think we have come into the gathering of the souls of these just men made perfect? Think about the money he used—the time, the skill, the energy, and the emotions. Do you think he had people paying tithe and buying his songs and messages because he wanted to eat? Did anyone pay him? The people enjoyed banquets and parties and weddings right up to the time Noah entered his boat, yet this man was spending his resources on an ark. Do we see the folly of our modern ministers who are paid thousands of pounds and dollars to come and minister? Do we see our folly when we sit to write and produce tapes and CDs and all that is in our mind is how they will sell? We are not yet moved with fear. When we are moved with fear, the love of Christ will constrain us; our passion will force us to reject all benefits and preach this message, not for profit. How fearful it is to fall into the hands of the living God. Noah, the preacher of righteousness, sacrificed his life just to save eight people. Indeed, we are of more value than many sparrows.

What is the conclusion of the long talk about money in the church? As church members, we should give to the poor and the needy (including ministers if they are in need). Whether you give 10 per cent or 100 per cent is your choice. You must give according to your ability. To whom much is given, much is expected. As ministers, let us know who is working for money or who is ministering for God. You cannot do both. As a church, let us spend our money for the right thing: humanity. Let us as a church not let money distract us from preaching holiness, without which no man will see God.

3

Will He find faith on the earth when He returns?

3.1 Introduction

This part sums up the role of Christians in society. It attempts to shed light on how we are meant to live in this world. Why are we as Christians exposed to the daily struggles of life and not taken straight away to heaven? Why will he not bring us into the many mansions in the Father's house? The simple answer is that we have a role to play in His kingdom—indeed, in this world. This is the discussion in this final part. Sadly, our home front and our church front are failing us. We do not encourage the right doctrine about our homes, because most ministers are increasingly chasing money.

3.2 Light and Salt

You are the salt of the earth. But if the salt loses its salty taste, it cannot be made salty again. It is good for nothing. It must be thrown out for people to walk on.
You are the light that gives light to the world. A city that is built on a hill cannot be hidden. And people don't hide a light under a bowl. They put the light on a lampstand. Then the light shines for all the people in the house. In the same way, you should be a light for other people. Live so that they will see the good things you do. Live so that they will praise your Father in heaven. (Matt. 5:13-16 ICB)

These two statements of Jesus' sum up the role of Christians on Earth. As a young man, I always wondered why we are not just taken away to heaven when we are saved. This passage is the reason. We are to show the standard of morality and character in this world. We are to preserve spirit, values, and goodwill until He returns. It is not politics. It is not wealth. Jesus did not need to die to put a man in government or make a man rich. David became king not through the cross. Solomon was rich not through Calvary. Did we get our salvation by vows and tithes? Did He decide to die and take our place because we formed cults and sects to take up political positions as a church? Is it not clear how much we have lost our cutting edge? While the early Christians sold and gave and the Holy Spirit was moving, we are claiming breakthroughs and wealth, and nothing is happening. In fact, nothing can happen if we continue like this. We need to tell ourselves repeatedly why we are still alive: to be light and salt.

Where is our strength of character as Christians? Where is the cutting edge? The world still knows the standard. They know we are not up to it. In every society, race, colour, or creed, I believe the standard of right and wrong is known. We know what light is to darkness. It has nothing to do with age, sex, or status. Jesus says to let your light shine. It is not in the laws. The laws say that thou shall not kill. The standard says do not even hate in your heart. It is not in the seen; it is in the unseen heart. All actions are weighed in the heart. It is everywhere. It is every time. It is everyone.

If you think of yourself as *rich*, the Bible says this:

> *Give this command to those who are rich with things of this world. Tell them not to be proud. Tell them to hope in God, not their money. Money cannot be trusted, but God takes care of us richly. He gives us everything to enjoy. Tell the rich people to do good and to be rich in doing good deeds. Tell them to be happy to give and ready to share.* (1 Tim. 6:17–18 ICB)

To the *slaves* it says,

> *Slaves, obey your masters here on earth with fear and respect. And do that with a heart that is true, just as you obey Christ. You must do more than obey your masters to please them only while they are*

watching you. You must obey them as you are obeying Christ. With all your heart you must do what God wants. (Eph. 6:5-6 ICB)

To *masters* it says,

Masters, in the same way, be good to your slaves. Do not say things to scare them. You know that the One who is your Master and their Master is in heaven. And that Master treats everyone alike. (Eph. 6:9 ICB)

To *children* it says,

Children, obey your parents the way the Lord wants. This is the right thing to do. The command says, "Honor your father and mother." This is the first command that has a promise with it. The promise is: "Then everything will be well with you, and you will have a long life on the earth." (Eph. 6:1-3 ICB)

To *fathers* it says,

Fathers, do not make your children angry, but raise them with the training and teaching of the Lord. (Eph. 6:4 ICB)

To all *citizens* it says,

All of you must obey the government rulers. No one rules unless God has given him the power to rule. And no one rules now without that power from God. (Rom. 13:1 ICB)

To the *ruler* it says,

He is God's servant to help you. But if you do wrong, then be afraid. The ruler has the power to punish; he is God's servant to punish those who do wrong. (Rom. 13:4 ICB)

To the *pastor* it says,

And a servant of the Lord must not quarrel! He must be kind to everyone. He must be a good teacher. He must be patient. The Lord's servant must gently teach those who do not agree with him. Maybe God will let them change their hearts so that they can accept the truth. (2 Tim. 24-25 ICB)

An elder must be so good that people cannot rightly criticize him. He must have only one wife. He must have self-control and be wise. He must be respected by other people and must be ready to help people by accepting them into his home. He must be a good teacher. He must not drink too much wine, and he must not be a man who likes to fight. He must be gentle and peaceful. He must not love money. He must be a good leader of his own family so that his children obey him with full respect. (If a man does not know how to be a leader over his own family, he will not be able to take care of God's church.) But an elder must not be a new believer. A new believer might be too proud of himself. Then he would be judged guilty for his pride just as the devil was. An elder must also have the respect of people who are not in the church. Then he will not be criticized by others and caught in the devil's trap. (1 Tim. 3:2-7 ICB)

To the *oppressor* it says,

The people asked John, "What should we do?"
John answered, "If you have two shirts, share with the person who does not have one. If you have food, share that too."
Even tax collectors came to John to be baptized. They said to John, "Teacher, what should we do?"
John said to them, "Don't take more taxes from people than you have been ordered to take."
The soldiers asked John, "What about us? What should we do?"
John said to them, "Don't force people to give you money. Don't lie about them. Be satisfied with the pay you get." (Luke 3:10-14 ICB)

We can go on and on about everyone in the Bible. Directly or indirectly, your person, position, or career is mentioned in the Bible. To the youths, it says to be an example of youths. To the husbands, it says to love your wives. There is a standard for everyone. In our generation, we may try to water it down. We as Christians are supposed to be examples. We are supposed to be preserving this earth. Sin may continue to increase. We are supposed to preserve the standards of God. We need to contend for the faith that was once delivered to the saints. We know what is right. I am not talking about religion here, I am talking about humanity. Good and evil. Truth and lie. Right and wrong. Why do we not have a breed of Christians who stand by the truth? The answer is simple: for so many years now, all we have emphasized in the church is prosperity. Therefore, we have lost grip of the real thing. The light must shine in darkness. Today we are only Christians on Sundays and light up only inside the church. Even this is dim because we are quarrelling over tables rather than teaching the word of God. Christianity is doing what is right, what is correct, what is fair before God and man. We must be known for truth.

Let us be known and remembered for the truth. When you imagine the apostle Paul in his writings (in his days when masters took slaves as commodities and wives were servants) preaching equality of all men, what goes on in your mind? Christianity is a movement. It is not for political attainments or financial gains. It is a movement of truth. It is not about activism and breaking people's glass or exhuming people from graves. It is doing what is right before God and man—loving your neighbour, doing good to all men, living at peace with all men, and owing no man anything but love. It is about giving to any man that asks of you. It is forgiving and trusting.

The total message is love, peace, and joy. Knowing we have a cloud of witnesses around us, knowing we have come into the gathering of souls of just men made perfect, we keep the standards. We keep the values. We show the way. We fight the fight. We finish the race. We keep the faith.

My heart quivers whenever I read of people in the Bible challenging men to condemn them if they can. It is not the challenge; it is the fact that people could not condemn them. Daniel for example, was involved in politics. His was not dirty. His was not deceitful. The Bible says opposition parties could not find anything to accuse him of—no document, no deals, no offence to nail him with. On the other hand, Samuel was in the church. He said before everyone, 'I have not taken anyone's goat or sheep nor cheated anyone.' These are shining examples. So it does not matter whether you are in the church, in business, or in politics. What matters is if you are standing by what Christianity stands for: the truth. Fewer and fewer people are willing to stand by the truth for fear of losing promotions, money, jobs, and so on. This is why this generation is losing the cutting edge as Christians.

Let us go ahead and talk more about generation and transfer of strength of character. Then we will ask ourselves again if we have any to transmit to the next generation.

3.3　Bad children

We shall endeavour in this chapter to outline the effects of not being able to transfer God's values to our children.

> Cain said to his brother Abel, "Let's go out into the field." So Cain and Abel went into the field. Then Cain attacked his brother Abel and killed him. (Gen. 4:8 ICB)

> Adam had sexual relations with his wife Eve again. And she gave birth to a son. She named him Seth. Eve said, "God has given me another child. He will take the place of Abel, who was killed by Cain." (Gen. 4:25 ICB)

We all have different tendencies as individuals. We also can be influenced by others. Many preachers have come up with so many stories about Cain and Abel. I do not intend to hatch another. We can stick to these facts in these passages. It was bad for a brother to rise up against another brother. Cain was so mad at both humans and God. This is just like the devil. Little wonder, therefore, that God said,

> "If you do good, I will accept you. But if you do not do good, sin is ready to attack you. Sin wants you. But you must rule over it." (Gen. 4:7 ICB)

We must conquer sin. If we do not, we will continue to have grief and sorrow like Adam and Eve, for our loved ones will always be no more. We will continue to look for replacement of lost opportunities. We may not be able to blame Adam or Eve for not raising up a good child. However, we know the effects of having a bad one: you lose the good ones as well.

Let us look at another example in Genesis 25. This story talks about children who brought trouble. Dinah, not thinking properly, took a walk in the neighbourhood. She went to see the daughters of the land. I have met many Christian women who believe that the 'free' women are enjoying their lives. The truth is that you are not in their shoes. We need to address the mind and behaviour rather than acts. What was in Dinah's mind when she went out? Whether we know why she went out or not, we are sure in retrospect that she should not have gone out. I do not think she was a good friend after the dust settled. I am sure she never went out afterward.

Shechem, on the other hand, cannot claim love and willingness to pay any price, if he could not pay the noble price of self-restrict. He could have gone along the normal path for what he thought he needed. Perhaps, like the father, the love of possessions impaired his judgement. The reason given to drive his point home was access to Jacobs's cattle and sheep. This child was taught what 1 John 2 says it is in this world:

> These are the evil things in the world: wanting things to please our sinful selves, wanting the sinful things we see, being too proud of the things we have. But none of those things comes from the Father. All of them come from the world. (1 John 2:16 ICB)

The craze for sex, the ambition to buy everything that appeals to you, and the pride that comes from wealth and importance—these are not from God. They are from this evil world itself.

Thank God for His mercies. If the Lord really does not keep us, we would be consumed. The Lord kept this family after this wicked act. The children of Jacob killed the men. Revenge! God will help us to teach our children that when we can turn the other cheek, it is a sign of strength. The effects of not teaching the next generation can bring about death in the family, in the country, or even in the world.

We have yet another example of bad children bringing disaster to a race. Let us look at the following:

> *Now Eli's sons were evil men. They did not care about the Lord. (1 Sam. 2:12 ICB)*

> *Now Eli was very old. He heard about everything his sons were doing to all the Israelites. He also heard about how his sons had sexual relations with the women who served at the entrance to the Meeting Tent. Eli said to his sons, "The people here tell me about the evil you do. Why do you do these evil things? No, my sons. The Lord's people are saying bad things about you. If someone sins against another person, God can help him. But if he sins against the Lord himself, no one can help him!" But Eli's sons would not listen to him. This was because the Lord had decided to put them to death. (1 Sam. 2:22-25 ICB)*

> *So why don't you respect the sacrifices and gifts? You honor your sons more than me. You become fat on the best parts of the meat the Israelites bring to me. (1 Sam. 2:29 ICB)*

From these passages, we can see how priests' children were totally disrespectful to God. We deceive ourselves by thinking we can preserve our faith by talk. We see how Eli talked to the sons. It is easy to say that the children were grown up and he was old; therefore, he could not do much more than just talk. However, further scrutiny reveals exactly what the problem was. Actions speak louder than many voices. God is accusing even Eli of fattening himself up upon the choicest parts of every offering of the people of Israel. Eli was a 'heavy' man and old when he fell and died.

> *And it came to pass, when he made mention of the ark of God, that he fell from off the seat backward by the side of the gate, and his neck brake, and he died: for he was an old man, and heavy. And he had judged Israel forty years (1 Sam. 4:18 KJV)*

How could he be part of the feast and then expect his children to listen and obey his hypocritical old voice?

The Bible says that the sons did not care about God. This is exactly our problem today. Our children do not care about God, because they do not see us challenging them with our lifestyles of truth and sincerity. When people do not see God in our actions, how do we expect them to believe in God? It is not so much what we say. It is not in the noises we make. It is in what we do. The church cannot be eating from corrupt people and then fighting corruption. The church cannot be accepting all sorts of funds and at the same time preaching holiness. Eli was eating from this same ill-gotten food and wealth; therefore, he had no moral grounds to query the children. Do we not see why churches have turned into pubs? Do we not see why our children do not care about God? We as Christians are not living out the truth and holiness of the scriptures. Maybe we should reflect on the results of this. The family lost its blessing. Both Eli and the sons died. Above all, a nation lost the ark of covenant: the presence of God. This is what we get when we do not train our children by our acts of sincerity and truth. With the state we are in today as Christians, we really wonder if He has not left us for a long time. We see why Jesus wondered if he would find faith on the Earth when He comes. Am I saying that once you are good, then your children will be good? No. However, we must do our part of standing by the truth and teaching it. Our children may learn from us. They may not learn, but they will have the standard. We will at least know we finished our own race. A good example is Samuel. Samuel grew up knowing the punishment to Eli and his sons. He grew up in the church. He lived a holy life. Oh, he did! He challenged people to accuse him of a fault. Yet the Bible says his sons were not like their father.

> His first son was named Joel, and his second son was named Abijah.
> Joel and Abijah were judges in Beersheba. But Samuel's sons did not
> live as he did. They tried to get money dishonestly. They took money
> secretly to be dishonest in their judging. (1 Sam. 8:2 ICB)

It is clear that Samuel showed them God's standards, but the children chose their lifestyle. I may not be able to say here what percentage of the blame goes to the parents and children in the lifestyle children eventually choose. Yet I can say that parents must play their part by showing good examples. After all, the testimony will be that the children are different from the parents. Having said that, I must say we cannot undermine our influence on our children. Whereas the issue of human choice is complex, we must be sure we have done our best. Anyhow, we can see clearly the consequences of bad children: national revolt against God. This reinforces why we must restructure our child evangelism in the church. It is a battle we must win by talking and by being good examples.

We can go on to talk about the family of David and the resultant incest, murder, and loss of his throne. We see Solomon too, and how his children divided the tribe of Israel into two kingdoms. Also, we have Hezekiah children, which eventually led to the exile of a nation. We can go on and on about bad children and the resultant individual or national sufferings. In all these, we can only reach the conclusion that we must do all we can to make sure we do not have bad children: pray all we can, talk all we can, live as right as we can, and teach all we can.

3.4 *Good children*

In this chapter, we shall talk about the exact opposite: good children and the blessings of having them.

Let us start by looking at some passages:

> *If the Lord doesn't build the house, the builders are working for nothing. If the Lord doesn't guard the city, the guards are watching for nothing. It is no use for you to get up early and stay up late, working for a living. The Lord gives sleep to those he loves. Children are a gift from the Lord. Babies are a reward. Sons who are born to a young man are like arrows in the hand of a warrior.* (Pss. 127:1-4 ICB)

> *Some people brought their small children to Jesus so he could touch them. But his followers told the people to stop bringing their children to him. When Jesus saw this, he was displeased. He said to them,*

"Let the little children come to me. Don't stop them. The kingdom of God belongs to people who are like these little children. I tell you the truth. You must accept the kingdom of God as a little child accepts things, or you will never enter it." Then Jesus took the children in his arms. He put his hands on them and blessed them. (Mark 10:13-16 ICB)

The Lord said, "Should I tell Abraham what I am going to do now? Abraham's children will certainly become a great and powerful nation. And all nations on earth will be blessed through him. I have chosen him so he would command his children and his descendants to live the way the Lord wants them to. I did this so they would live right and be fair. Then I, the Lord, will give Abraham what I promised him."

Then the Lord said, "I have heard many things against the people of Sodom and Gomorrah. They are very evil. (Gen. 18:17-20 ICB)

We see here one advantage of having good children: God becomes much closer. We have deeper understanding or knowledge of things. We even have a chance to turn the fate of others. What more do we want in life?

Another example of the benefit of having good children can be found in the book of Exodus. It is about the story of a family.

Amram's wife was named Jochebed. She was from the tribe of Levi. She was born in Egypt. She and Amram had two sons, Aaron and Moses, and their sister Miriam. (Num. 26:59 ICB)

This family is an unparalleled one when it comes to child evangelism.

This woman, Jochebed, born in Egypt, grew up and raised a family that shook Egypt to its foundation. Her family hid a baby for three months. The daughter would not let the basket out of her sight. The same daughter had enough social and mental strength to engage the king's daughter in a persuasive conversation. The mum was called to take care of the baby for some time. This baby was handed to the palace with all sorts of worldly attractions: wealth, fame, and women. Yet in the end, this same boy chose the way of God over thrones, kingdoms, and fame. Then we read of the older brother being a mouthpiece, saying exactly what God says. No propaganda. Just His words. They led a nation out of bondage. They had some misunderstanding that delayed movement for a few days. Even in it, the love and bond were so strong that God had to use His veto power to make the sister remain in her state for the few days.

Anytime we look at this family, we cannot help but wonder how this happened. What was it that the parents taught their children? Even more baffling is what they must have told baby Moses that kept his heart fixed on God in the palace as he grew up. As family men, I like us to pause, walk over to our children, and imagine we have only today with them and then we may never see them again. Talk to them. Pray for them. This is but a glimpse of the heart burden of the parents in this story, for in their case they indeed lived every day as the last with their baby. Do we see where the bond came from?

Let me ask a disturbing question: what gives us the guarantee that we will see our children tomorrow when we wish them good night? If only we could just take one day as another opportunity to show that child the love of God. In our smiles, in our handshakes, in our hugs, or even in our punishment, we will be raising future leaders in God's great army. If we were going to die today, do we really think we would not tell our children about heaven and hell?

Timothy is another example of a child that was brought up well.

> *I remember that you cried for me. And I want very much to see you so that I can be filled with joy. I remember your true faith. That kind of faith first belonged to your grandmother Lois and to your mother Eunice. And I know that you now have that same faith. That is why I remind you to use the gift God gave you. God gave you that gift when I laid my hands on you. Now let it grow, as a small flame grows into a fire. (2 Tim. 1:4-6 ICB)*

The Bible speaks of Timothy as a man with sincere faith. It speaks of it as a family thing. Oh, that we are able to pass on our sincere faith unto our children. When we realise that the things of God are not hereditary, when we realise that every man must work out his salvation with fear and trembling, then we know these parents worked to preserve these values. We may never be able to guess how they did it, but we know that the result was Timothy having *true faith*. Indeed, in these last days, when we must serve God in spirit and in truth. A pastor once said that he could not afford to give birth to a child who would increase the number of people in hell. All we need is to burn the light in our own little corner. We must serve God in genuineness. A tree will always bring forth after its own kind. Jesus said that if we abide, our fruits will abide. We want our families to be Christians.

There are many other good lads in the Bible. We have Samuel, Daniel, Shedrach, Meshach, and Abednego. We also have Rhoda and the little boy with the fish and bread that Jesus used to feed thousands. In all these examples, we see as parents that we must work on our children by exemplary living and by instructions to make them know God. It is vital that instructions and living by example align.

3.5   Conclusion

What do we see today in our churches? Children come into the church full of prosperity messages. Sometimes all they can do is play games, paint, and draw. Of course, they do not understand the message of breakthrough and abundance yet. They get back home and continue with the games, painting, and drawing—not to mention television watching. We must do more than this. We must train up our children in the way they should go. Jesus wondered if there would be faith on Earth when He comes back. Fashion will continue to grow wild. Sensual behaviour will keep on rising. We know that the Bible says there is nothing new under the sun. We know sin is not only with our generation. Right now, sin is escalating.

Jesus' words must be taken more seriously.

> *You are the world's seasoning, to make it tolerable. If you lose your flavor, what will happen to the world? And you yourselves will be thrown out and trampled underfoot as worthless. You are the world's*

light—a city on a hill, glowing in the night for all to see (Matt. 5:13-14 TLB)

As a church (and as individuals), we must decide to preserve the earth and show good spirit. We must focus on the right issues of holiness and strength of character and bring our children up to Christ for laying on of hands and for blessing. Otherwise we will continue to lose our buildings to pubs and cinemas. We must go back to the values of Christianity: holiness and humanity.

We know what is right by the text of the scriptures. Gone are the days when music composers write about 'Stand up for Jesus'. What we hear now is, 'We worship you; we love you.' We sing what we do not mean. How can we worship God? According to Jesus, we worship in spirit and in truth with sincerity of purpose. How do we love God? Again, according to Jesus we love by keeping His commandments. We claim that we love him, yet we cannot obey Him in public. How can we be talking about divorce and sexual perversions inside the church among ministers? I have carefully listened to arguments by these people on TV. The summary is that it is their makeup or nature. I wonder if there is any sin that we do not like or that is not our nature. Maybe we should begin to allow, in the church, other sins like killing, paedophile, adultery, and so forth, because the adults involved like it.

How can we as Christians claim social security allowances based on lies we have told? How can we be living and working based on falsified immigration papers and then claim that we are Christians?

The Bible says that we are the standard. We are the light. We cannot be living a lie or lying to live. Indeed, hell is expanding its boundaries. My heart sobs for the next generation. If in our generation, money matter beclouds right teachings, one wonders what the next generation will be like.

We must make sacrifices to shine. We must burn to shine. We must heat up to shine. We must collide to shine. We must lose energy to shine. All the same, we must decide to shine. Look at a street with street lights. They are scattered—not covering every inch. Yet that is just enough to light up everywhere. You are the only Christian in your company; you are there to shine. Shine your little light. In that little corner of yours, shine your little light. That is all that is needed. When you shine and I shine, just like the street light, we may just light up the whole street.

Paul said:

> I have fought the good fight, I have finished the race, I have kept the faith. (2 Tim. 4:7 NIV)

First we have a calling to keep being Christians. As Christians, we must be able to keep ourselves under, less we become cast away. Then we have a part to play in the church. We have our roles. We have a position that we must occupy. Then we have a responsibility for the body of Christ. We must make sure that the faith we are leaving behind is the one that was handed over to us. We must make sure that in that part we played, we held the faith. We contributed positively to His body. We must leave the stage handing over the faith that was handed over to us.